ISSUES THAT CONCERN YOU

Alcoholism

Tamara L. Roleff, *Book Editor*

GREENHAVEN PRESS
A part of Gale, Cengage Learning

GALE
CENGAGE Learning

Detroit • New York • San Francisco • New Haven, Conn • Waterville, Maine • London

Christine Nasso, *Publisher*
Elizabeth Des Chenes, *Managing Editor*

© 2010 Greenhaven Press, a part of Gale, Cengage Learning

Gale and Greenhaven Press are registered trademarks used herein under license.

For more information, contact:
Greenhaven Press
27500 Drake Rd.
Farmington Hills, MI 48331-3535
Or you can visit our Internet site at gale.cengage.com

For product information and technology assistance, contact us at

Gale Customer Support, 1-800-877-4253
For permission to use material from this text or product, submit all requests online at www.cengage.com/permissions

Further permissions questions can be e-mailed to permissionrequest@cengage.com

Articles in Greenhaven Press anthologies are often edited for length to meet page requirements. In addition, original titles of these works are changed to clearly present the main thesis and to explicitly indicate the author's opinion. Every effort is made to ensure that Greenhaven Press accurately reflects the original intent of the authors. Every effort has been made to trace the owners of copyrighted material.

Cover image copyright Deklofenak, 2010. Used under license from Shutterstock.com.

LIBRARY OF CONGRESS CATALOGING-IN-PUBLICATION DATA

Alcoholism / Tamara L. Roleff, book editor.
    p. cm. -- (Issues that concern you)
  Includes bibliographical references and index.
  ISBN 978-0-7377-4742-3 (hbk.)
1. Alcoholism--Juvenile literature. 2. Drinking of alcoholic beverages--Juvenile literature. I. Roleff, Tamara L., 1959-
  HV5066.A396 2010
  616.86'1--dc22
                                                            2009050760

Printed in the United States of America
  2 3 4 5 6 7 14 13 12 11 10

CONTENTS

When alcoholics and people who abuse alcohol want to stop or cut back on their drinking, they generally do not change their drinking behavior because they no longer enjoy the taste of alcohol. Indeed, most people who drink do so because they like the taste of alcohol, whether it is beer, wine, or hard liquor, and they like how drinking makes them feel. However, they have found that their drinking is causing problems for them, perhaps in their social life, with their family, or at school or work. Perhaps a husband is upset about how much his wife is drinking while she is preparing dinner, a girlfriend is unhappy about how often her boyfriend goes out drinking with his friends, or a teacher or boss notices that a student or employee often comes to school or work drunk. Many people who abuse alcohol deny that they are alcoholics or that they have a drinking problem, but the people who love them and work with them disagree. A person may have an alcohol problem even if he or she is not addicted to alcohol. Michael S. Levy, a psychiatrist and director of an addiction treatment center, tells his clients, "If your drinking causes you and others around you serious difficulties, you have an alcohol use problem."[1]

Alcoholism is a chronic condition that will only get progressively worse if nothing is done to stop or control the drinking. Besides the disruptions to family and work life, alcoholics also suffer from liver diseases, heart problems, diabetes, and fatigue; are prone to accidents, mental health issues, suicides, and domestic violence problems; and often have run-ins with the law. Most physicians, therapists, and addiction counselors maintain that alcoholism is a disease and that the only way to recover from it is to stop drinking completely. Treatment options include quitting "cold turkey" on one's own, attending support groups such as Alcoholics Anonymous for help in staying sober, seeing a counselor for help in changing the way the alcoholic thinks about alcohol, entering a residential treatment center for intensive care

Abusing alcohol can lead to a host of problems, including disruptions in family relationships.

and therapy for one to three months (or longer), and taking drugs that will cause severe reactions when alcohol is consumed.

Some alcoholics and alcohol abusers attempt another option: moderated drinking. Adherents of moderated drinking believe that alcoholism is not a disease but a learned behavior. The difference between alcoholism being considered a disease and a learned behavior is an important distinction. According to Levy, "If problem drinking is learned, it may be possible for some people to learn how to moderate their drinking."[2] He goes on to cite different ways in which people can change their drinking habits. For example, problem drinkers may decide to limit their drinking to only holidays or special occasions, totally abstain for a specific time period before starting to drink again in moderation, limit their drinking to only a few drinks on weekends or a few days a week, drink only in social settings where they know they will not overdo it, or change the type of alcohol they drink. Levy maintains that the most important fact is not what aspect of their drinking behavior that problem drinkers are changing but "the simple fact that they are *able* to do this." He stresses, however, that because the causes of alcoholism are complex (Is it caused by biological, psychological, or cultural factors, perhaps a combination of all three, or even something else?), "it is shortsighted and narrow-minded to think that there is only one way to understand a person's problem with alcohol."[3]

Alcoholics Anonymous (AA), probably the best-known and most popular self-help group for alcoholics in the world, is firm in its stance on alcohol. According to AA, alcoholism is a disease. Moreover, alcoholics cannot live a sober life until they acknowledge that they are "powerless over alcohol" and that their "lives had become unmanageable."[4] AA supporters are also convinced that no one can fully recover from alcoholism until he or she has "hit bottom,"[5] although one alcoholic's definition of hitting bottom may be vastly different from another's definition. But perhaps most important of all, recovering alcoholics at AA believe the only treatment that works is abstinence, not limiting or moderating their drinking. Jack H. Hedblom, a psychotherapist and author of *Last Call: Alcoholism and Recovery*, writes: "Attempts at controlled drinking do not work; things just get worse. The alcoholic cannot drink. At the meetings one hears over and over . . . 'It is the first drink that gets you drunk.'"[6]

The debate over whether alcoholics can relearn how to drink is relevant to the entire debate over alcoholism itself: Is it a disease or a behavior; must alcoholics be abstinent for the rest of their lives; are binge drinkers alcoholics or in danger of becoming alcoholics; and what treatment programs are effective in helping alcoholics take control of their lives again? The articles in this anthology present a wide range of opinion on the many controversies surrounding alcoholism.

Notes

1. Michael S. Levy, *Take Control of Your Drinking . . . and You May Not Need to Quit*. Baltimore: Johns Hopkins University Press, 2009, p. 12.

2. Levy, *Take Control of Your Drinking*, pp. 25–26.

3. Levy, *Take Control of Your Drinking*, p. 26.

4. Alcoholics Anonymous, *Twelve Steps and Twelve Traditions*. New York: AA Grapevine, 2007, p. 21.

5. Alcoholics Anonymous, *Twelve Steps and Twelve Traditions*, p. 24.

6. Jack H. Hedblom, *Last Call: Alcoholism and Recovery*. Baltimore: Johns Hopkins University Press, 2009, p. 19.

ONE

Alcoholism Is a Disease

Mark Lender

> In the following viewpoint Mark Lender, a professor of history at Kean University, discusses the characteristics that qualify alcoholism as a disease. Lender claims that although alcohol abuse was once viewed as a moral failing, it is in fact a disease qualified by four major characteristics. Over the years, research has shown that not only do environmental factors play a role in a person developing alcoholism, but heredity also can be a factor.

From the jiggers of whiskey downed by the dozens in ill-lit Old West frontier bars to the government-evading moonshiners plying their trade in the deep hickory woods on the flanks of the Appalachians, alcohol has been an integral part of America's lore.

But the romantic, devil-may-care aura surrounding this significant component of our culture is overshadowed by the fact that alcohol is a primary cause of 100,000 deaths a year in the United States, about one-fourth of all hospital admissions, and $166 billion in annual economic losses.

Although a majority of Americans enjoy drinking and successive generations have incorporated some degree of alcohol use into their lives, many have found it to also be a source of health problems, addiction, social disruption, and personal tragedy. Today, perhaps 14 million Americans (about 1 in every 13 adults) have some magnitude of a drinking problem, and around 8 million are actual full-blown alcoholics.

According to the National Institute on Alcohol Abuse and Alcoholism (NIAAA), part of the National Institutes of Health, over half of the U.S. population has family members or close relatives with drinking problems. In fact, problem drinking is one of the most enduring social and health issues in American history.

Alcoholism Is a Disease, Not a Vice

Alcoholism defies easy definition. As early as the 1780s, some physicians considered it a disease and, while not using the term, an addiction. The classic statement on the subject was An Inquiry Into the Effects of Ardent Spirits on the Human Mind and Body (1784), by Benjamin Rush of Philadelphia. Rush was perhaps America's foremost physician, and he had no quarrel with beers and wines, which he believed healthful in moderation, but he argued that "ardent spirits" (distilled liquor) could eventually cause illness and death.

He called chronic drunkenness a disease that led drinkers through an addiction process, and he identified alcohol as the addictive agent. Once an "appetite" for spirits had become fixed, Rush claimed, drunkenness was not a vice, for the imbiber had lost control over drinking. Instead, the alcohol controlled the drinker.

With differences in detail, this disease conception has survived into the present. The modern definition of alcoholism also includes four key components.

- One is physical dependence, characterized by withdrawal symptoms following episodes of heavy drinking. When he stops drinking, the alcoholic can suffer from shakes, nausea, agitation, sweating, or combinations of these symptoms.
- Another element is craving (Rush's "appetite"), the compulsion to drink.
- This is coupled with loss of control, the inability of a drinker to stop drinking once started.

- Finally, tolerance is the alcoholic's need for larger quantities of alcohol in order to feel its effects.

In the current definition of alcoholism—as in Rush's formulation—the inability to control the need for alcohol is the crucial factor. Willpower has little chance in the face of craving or loss of control.

Yet most problem drinkers are not alcoholics. They may drive while under the influence, miss work or lose friends because of their drinking, or experience alcohol-related health or other difficulties. These are serious matters; if drinking behavior involves any of them within a single year, some authorities define it as alcohol abuse, which has created as much concern as alcoholism.

In the nineteenth century, many business managers became temperance advocates after seeing alcohol's impact on safety in the industrial workplace. Henry Ford, a prohibitionist at one point in his career, did not believe that drinking could coexist with operating automobiles. Indeed, the public safety aspect of alcohol abuse remains an important issue quite apart from the matter of alcoholism; witness the modern activities of Mothers Against Drunk Driving.

Alcohol abuse can involve some signs of tolerance. But without craving, loss of control, and dependence, problem drinking—as dangerous as it may be—is not actual alcoholism.

Causes of Alcoholism

Since at least the era of Rush, medical, scientific, and other concerned parties have probed the roots of this disease, with a particular emphasis on the addictive nature of alcohol. They have understood that, at some point, an alcoholic simply loses the ability to stop drinking. But why? Aside from moralistic explanations popular among early reformers, the chief focus of many researchers has been heredity.

Since at least the nineteenth century, many writers noted that alcohol problems seemed to run in families. In the late 1800s, the Association for the Study and Cure of Inebriety, comprising mostly doctors and asylum managers, believed that alcohol

Regions of the Human Brain That Are Vulnerable to Alcoholism-Related Abnormalities

People who have been drinking large amounts of alcohol for long periods of time run the risk of developing serious and persistent changes in the brain. Damage may be a result of the direct effects of alcohol on the brain or may result indirectly, from a poor general health status or from severe liver disease. Long-term heavy drinking may lead to shrinking of the brain and deficiencies in the fibers that carry information between brain cells. Studies with animals show that high doses of alcohol lead to a disruption in the growth of new brain cells. Scientists believe it may be this lack of new growth that results in the long-term deficits found in key areas of the brain (such as hippocampal structure and function).

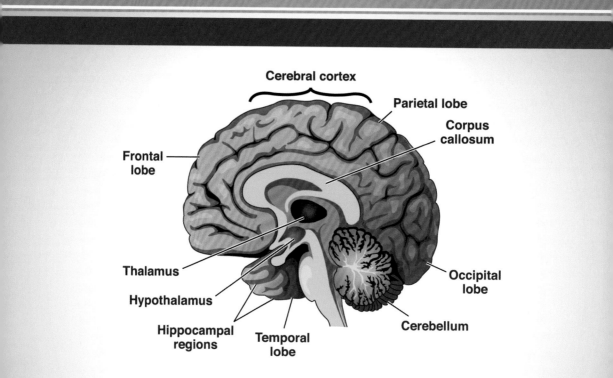

Taken from: National Institute on Alcohol Abuse and Alcoholism, "Alcohol's Damaging Effects on the Brain," *Alcohol Alert*, October 2004.

changed human cell structure, which initiated craving and the transmission of the addiction to future generations. The science and its conclusions were wrong, but such early theories at least helped put alcoholism on the scientific agenda.

The modern alcohol research movement began in the early 1930s, with achievements in biotechnology and genetics allowing some of the most interesting advances in the last two decades. Significantly, genetic studies have indicated that there is a hereditary element in alcoholism. Perhaps 40 to 60 percent of alcoholism is due to genetic predisposition, and research efforts have focused intensively on identifying the specific genes involved. In the future, genetic engineering may make it possible to influence particular genetic traits that make individuals vulnerable.

While genetics may explain why certain individuals are especially vulnerable to alcoholism, it is not an absolute predictor. Environmental factors, including demographic, religious, social, and cultural influences, play a role. The drinking behavior of family, friends, or religious or ethnic groups and the availability and price of alcohol can affect individual drinking patterns as well as local rates of alcoholism and alcohol abuse.

Few researchers expect any single causal model of alcoholism to emerge, and thus, in the end, the interaction of genetic and environmental factors is the favored explanation.

The Impact of Problem Drinking

Even today's relatively low consumption levels carry a cost, part of which is measured in health problems. Abusive drinking can harm almost every bodily system: It increases the risk of heart disease and cancer, especially in the mouth, throat, and upper digestive tract. It reduces the efficiency of the immune system, leaving problem drinkers more vulnerable to infectious diseases, and it is the leading cause of liver diseases, particularly cirrhosis. Alcohol is also a threat to the unborn: between 4,000 and 12,000 babies are born every year with symptoms of fetal alcohol syndrome.

Alcohol can be a killer. Problem drinking and alcoholism, according to the NIAAA, are primary factors in some 100,000 deaths each year. Additionally, they are complicating factors in over one-third of all deaths involving other nonmedical drugs (including illegal narcotics). In fact, alcohol ranks behind only tobacco and high-risk activities as the leading cause of preventable mortality, also accounting for about one-fourth of general hospital admissions every year. The health toll of drinking, then, is huge.

The impact of alcohol on families has been a long-standing concern. Over the late nineteenth and early twentieth centuries, for instance, the Women's Christian Temperance Union campaigned under the banner of "home protection," which struck a chord with thousands who had seen the drinking of breadwinners impoverish families or destroy them through alcohol-related domestic violence.

One does not have to agree with the aims of the temperance movement to appreciate the continuing importance of the issue. Current estimates indicate that over 1.5 million children have an alcoholic parent, while many studies have tied alcohol to a high proportion of child abuse, domestic violence cases, and broken marriages. The effect of problem drinking on the family is an age-old issue, but it is still very much with us.

Treating Alcoholism

There is no known cure for alcoholism. For the vast majority of alcoholics, the safest course is abstinence, which is the goal of most treatment efforts. In general, alcoholism seems to respond to treatment about as well as most chronic health disorders.

Once withdrawn from alcohol, and with proper social support, alcoholics can stay sober for years—indefinitely, if they remain abstinent. (Though there have been cases of diagnosed alcoholics returning to nonabusive drinking, treatments based on controlled drinking or other nonabstinence goals remain controversial.)

Most treatment takes place on an outpatient basis, but serious cases can require an institutional setting. After prolonged drinking, treatment usually involves detoxification, the process of ridding the body of alcohol. A number of drugs, notably disulfiram

Since alcohol abuse affects nearly every bodily system, it can lead to serious health problems—including death.

(marketed as Antabuse) and naltrexone (trademarked as ReVia), can help some alcoholics avoid relapsing. Virtually all treatment efforts involve some form of counseling to help alcoholics cope with their condition.

Treatment with Alcoholics Anonymous

Most treatment programs include participation in Alcoholics Anonymous (AA). Since its founding in 1935, the program has helped hundreds of thousands of alcoholics reach and maintain sobriety. AA calls itself a "worldwide fellowship of men and women who help each other to stay sober," and membership is open to all on a nonsectarian basis.

From the beginning, anonymity was the key to upholding the ideals embodied in the Twelve Steps, which offer participants a guide to coping with their own drinking and helping others. In AA's view, anonymity subordinated personalities to principles and avoided outside interference in the group's concerns. Regular meetings of local fellowships, which featured the personal stories of member alcoholics, served to assist participants in the practical application of the Twelve Steps.

Actually, AA's self-help idea was not new. As early as the 1840s, and continuing into the early 1900s, members of the Washington Temperance Society (usually called the "Washingtonians"), various reform clubs, and dry fraternal lodges (such as the Sons of Temperance) also used a mutual-assistance approach to sobriety. Like AA, these groups offered drinkers social stability, a common understanding of their powerlessness in the face of alcohol, group meetings, and assistance if they relapsed. These early self-help organizations aided thousands while they existed. Unlike AA, they failed to institutionalize successfully.

For all its accomplishments, however, AA has its critics. Its strong spiritual emphasis is not for everyone, and its insistence on abstinence has drawn fire as well.

Still other critics want the fellowship to drop its anonymity, arguing that AA members cannot serve as role models for recovery unless they are publicly visible. Early in its history, there were complaints that the group was oriented narrowly toward white, middle-class drinkers.

In response, AA can justifiably say that it never claimed that its approach was for everyone. Moreover, it would make little sense to give up anonymity: It has been one of AA's strongest attractions, and abandoning it for any reason would risk putting off many who otherwise would benefit from the organization. If the public needs role models, there are plenty of celebrity alcoholics who regularly bring their stories to the media.

AA also has demonstrated an ability to broaden its base and now functions well among black, Hispanic, and other minority groups. Over time, it has consistently produced more impressive results than any other alcoholism treatment program, although it seems to work best in conjunction with other medical and counseling efforts.

Prevention

Prevention—stopping problems before they begin—has been another key element in efforts to deal with problem drinking. Rush's Inquiry was meant to change drinking behavior to reduce problems; and Prohibition, whatever else it was, was intended as the ultimate prevention policy. Modern prevention efforts are varied, incorporating legal initiatives, such as stricter DUI (driving under the influence) laws and requiring warning labels on liquor bottles, as well as educational measures, including alcohol education in the schools. But prevention efforts, especially education, seldom work quickly. (In fact, research has shown that some do not work at all or may actually raise youthful curiosity about alcohol and induce early drinking.)

Yet over the long term and in aggregate, many prevention measures do help. States that have lowered the legal blood alcohol concentration (BAC) from .10 to .08, for example, have seen fatal crashes among drivers with BACs above .08 decline by some 16 percent. Thirty-eight states can now revoke the driving privileges of unsafe drivers, including drunk drivers, without court hearings. In these states, fatal nighttime accidents have been reduced by 6 to 9 percent.

Raising the minimum drinking age to 21 has substantially reduced traffic fatalities. Various alcohol education programs have aimed to help students delay taking up drinking. This delay is critical, as research indicates that most individuals who escape drinking problems before 21 will likely never experience them.

Properly employed, then, prevention will remain an important part of the nation's effort to curb alcoholism and alcohol abuse.

TWO

Alcoholism Is Not a Disease

Gene Heyman, interviewed by Charlie Gillis

In the following viewpoint Charlie Gillis, a reporter for *Maclean's* magazine, interviews Gene Heyman, a psychologist, an associate professor at Harvard University, and the author of *Addiction: A Disorder of Choice*. Heyman argues that his research found that addiction is governed by personal choice and does not fit the clinical conception of an illness. Heyman contends that addicts—whether they are addicted to drugs or alcohol—are influenced by the same forces that have an effect on those who are not addicts. These forces can also influence addicts who want to stop using drugs. Heyman agrees that while no one chooses to be an addict, people continue to call addiction a disease because it seems to be a more humane thing to say.

The idea that addiction is a disease is an article of faith in the study of drug and alcohol dependence, providing the foundation for much of the treatment and public policy related to addiction since the early 1900s. In [his recent] book, psychologist Gene Heyman dismantles this time-honoured assumption, arguing that addiction is first and foremost governed by personal choice, and does not therefore fit clinical conceptions of behavioural illness. Heyman has done research on choice, cognition and drug use. He has done volunteer work at a methadone clinic and he currently teaches courses on addiction at Harvard University. In conversation with *Maclean's* correspondent Charlie Gillis, he offers a model of decision-making that he says explains how addicts—from smokers to opiate users—can voluntarily engage in activities that lead to long-term misery.

Charlie Gillis: *The title of your new book,* Addiction: A Disorder of Choice, *is more or less self-explanatory. What led you to think that addiction may not be, as most research literature describes it, a "chronic, relapsing disease?"*

Gene Heyman: Like everybody else, my initial goal was to find out how drug use turned from a voluntary behaviour to an involuntary one—that's what I put down on my grant applications. But when I was teaching, I wanted to give my students at least some feeling for what addiction is like. So I began reading biographies, histories and ethnographies of addiction. This data gave a very different picture than the one I expected. The literature on how addicted people behave showed they stopped using the drugs, and that they did so because of family issues, or there was a choice between their children and continued drug use, or they were moving on to an environment where it was disapproved of.

In other words, the kinds of things that influence all of our everyday decisions were influencing people who are heavy, heavy drug users to stop using. And it was so consistent. Each report supported the other.

Then I began looking at the epidemiological data—these large surveys that have formed the basis for a lot of important psychiatric research in the last 20 years—and they showed the same thing. A huge percentage of people who had at some point met the criteria for lifetime substance dependence no longer did so by the time they were in their 30s. It varied from 60 to 80 per cent.

So why does that preclude it from being a disease?

At the heart of the notion of behavioural disease is the idea of compulsivity, by which people mean it's beyond the influence of reward, punishment, expectations, cultural values, personal values. Alan Leshner [the former head of the National Institute on Drug Abuse] says drug use starts off as voluntary and becomes involuntary. But the epidemiological evidence suggests otherwise. When you read the biographical information, you see individual drug addicts [who've quit] saying, "Well, it was a question of getting high on cocaine or putting food on the table for my kids." Or, "My life was getting out of control." Or, in the case of [noted author] William S. Burroughs, "The cheques from my parents stopped coming."

The Idea That Addiction Is a Disease

How, then, did the idea that addiction is a disease governed by uncontrollable compulsion take root?

The first people to call addiction a disease were members of the 17th-century clergy. They were looking at alcoholism and they didn't describe it as sin or as crime. I have a theory as to why they thought this—and why we think it even today. It's this problem we have with the idea that individuals can voluntarily do themselves harm. It just doesn't make sense to us. Why wouldn't you stop? In the medical world, in economics, in psychology and in the clergy, they really have no category for this, no way of explaining behaviour that is self-destructive and also voluntary. The two categories available to them are "sick" or "bad."

With the scientific community behind it, the idea that addiction is a sickness has also become the more enlightened position.

Yes, it seems a more humane thing to say, and people like to be humane.

Problematic Research

At the centre of your argument is that much of the research on addiction to date is based on people who wound up in treatment clinics. Why is that problematic?

It's problematic because 60 to 70 per cent of the time, those people have additional psychiatric disorders. And those disorders interfere with their capacity to engage in activities that would compete with the drugs—jobs, family, other activities. So the people the clinicians see, and the people the researchers study, are those who keep using drugs and don't stop right into their 40s.

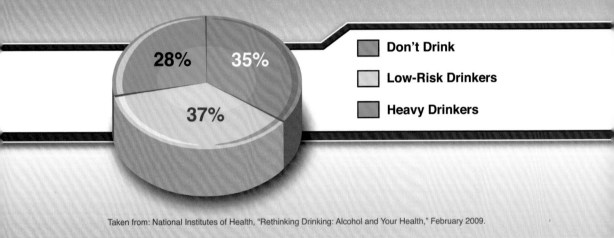

Alcohol Use by Adults in the United States

A nationwide survey of forty-three thousand American adults aged eighteen and older by the National Institutes of Health found that seven out of ten Americans either do not drink at all or drink at low-risk levels.

28% 35%

37%

- ■ Don't Drink
- □ Low-Risk Drinkers
- ■ Heavy Drinkers

Taken from: National Institutes of Health, "Rethinking Drinking: Alcohol and Your Health," February 2009.

That's maybe 15 to 20 per cent of [addicts], and they have greatly skewed our picture of the natural history of addiction. From the data I've seen, it looks like most people who meet the criteria for addiction actually stop using by age 30.

Why would respected and established scientists make generalizations about drug dependence based on such a small subset?

I've thought a lot about that, and my sense is that this subset fit what people believed before they started studying. It squares nicely with this notion that addiction was either bad behaviour or sick behaviour. I don't push this too hard. I mean, everybody knows that clinical populations can be biased. There's even a name for it—Berkson's bias. People who come to clinics for a certain disorder are likely to suffer from additional disorders.

Still, the broader epidemiological surveys you cite have been available for anyone who cared to look. Why do you think they were ignored?

Well, I only looked at this data because I was teaching this course. I felt I had to. If you're doing research looking at, say, calcium channels in individual neurons, you have so much to do that you're not going to start reading the epidemiological literature. You don't start making your world more difficult. But in the end, I do think it's inexcusable, and one of the goals of my book is to bring the research world's attention to data that has been sitting there for 20 years. In some cases, the data didn't fit in with what the people who sponsored the surveys say addiction is. The National Institute on Drug Abuse and National Institute on Alcohol Abuse and Alcoholism funded all the studies I cite. But NIDA and NIAAA have not taken the message of those studies to heart.

The Role of Choice

Let's talk about the role of choice in addiction. Your argument depends on the idea that a person can voluntarily engage in a behaviour that is self-destructive. Can you explain this phenomenon?

My analysis is based on the fact that there are always two "best" ways to make choices. We can take into consideration the value it has at the moment—the immediate rewards. Or we can consider this kind of circle of expanding consequences that each of our choices has. Your pattern of choices can be much different depending on whether you take into consideration this broader circle. A workaholic, for example, starts out taking into account only the immediate demands of working, dropping every other consideration. But he ends up, according to himself and everybody around him, working too much. The model just tries to formalize that idea, and it's really just common sense.

So when people are choosing the drug, they're thinking that moment, or that particular day, would be better if they did. A chronic smoker will think that the next three minutes would be better with a cigarette than without. But after a year of smoking 20 cigarettes per day, adding up to 60 minutes each day, you might think, 'I'd rather have the 60 minutes of not smoking each day.' Unfortunately, you don't choose 60 minutes at a time. You decide one cigarette—or three minutes—at a time, and that's what makes this so difficult.

So as we get older, we learn to recognize those consequences, and weigh them against other things we might spend our time on.

Right. Your preferences in the moment are different from what I'd call a global perspective, and they can undermine that global perspective. That's why I'm actually in favour of drug and alcohol treatment. Many of these programs help get people through the very difficult periods of choosing things in the moment, one at a time.

Implications of Heyman's Arguments

Your tone is even and your argument seems rational. But there are implications to all this. You're upending ideas that have had scientific currency since the First World War. Our governments spend billions each year treating and trying to prevent drug abuse on the belief it is a disease. Are we going about it all wrong?

My sense is that we could be going about it a lot better. It's possible that the reason we're not making much progress is that we're not treating decision-making directly. There are programs that have had considerable success, and they are based on the idea that the consequences of drug use are what's important. There is one for airline pilots and physicians where the success rates are 80 or 90 per cent abstinence, because the negative consequences are so serious [if they fail to abstain, the addicts lose their jobs].

It's harder where the subjects are unemployed, but again it points out the fact that this is a question of alternatives. If programs focused on alternatives, consequences and rewards in a very direct way, maybe they'd be much more efficacious and less expensive. . . .

No One Chooses to Be an Addict

We should probably make an important distinction here. While you call addiction a "disorder of choice," you also stress that no one chooses to be an addict. What do you mean by that?

That you're making these choices one day at a time. What you're choosing is to take heroin that day. You're not choosing to have a miserable life. Eventually, you become stuck, though,

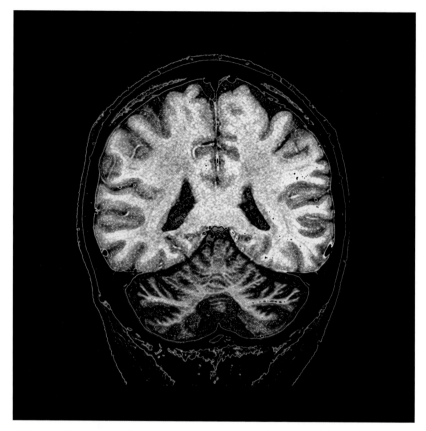

The author says that no one chooses to be an addict; nonetheless, the health consequences of alcohol abuse can be devastating. This color-enhanced magnetic resonance image of an alcoholic's brain displays atrophy of the cerebellum (in orange) caused by alcoholism.

where you don't know what else to do but choose heroin each day, even though you wish it didn't lead to a miserable life. You know, I've always thought it strange that people would think we should not have sympathy for those kinds of situations. In modern society, it is so easy to do things that you will later regret, whether we're talking about something you do on the computer or something that you put in your body. A lot of people have trouble not making the selfish decision—the one that ruins their lives and the lives of those around them—and some of these treatment programs can help them figure that out. I also think that's a reasonable thing for a clinician to want to do: to help people make better decisions about their lives.

The concept of safe injection sites for intravenous drug users has been a hot topic here in Canada. We had a pilot project in Vancouver, which aimed to reduce associated harms, like the spread of HIV [human immunodeficiency virus, which causes AIDS] or hepatitis. Critics of the concept say it sends the message that drug use is okay. What do you think?

I don't know that free needles will make someone a heroin addict. But would somebody say to themselves, "I don't need to quit if I can find a place to inject safely"? Yeah, they might.

There's also the matter of putting the imprimatur [approval] of government on something it supposedly disapproves of.

Yes, and I think those things can be pretty important. In the U.S., when the surgeon general's report came out in 1964 saying smoking was bad for your health, it had an impact. Everybody knew it couldn't be good for you. But when it became official, people actually began to stop smoking. So those are the sorts of things you would have to consider [regarding safe injection sites]; you would have to weigh them against the public health advantages, and I think it would be a very hard decision. It would take a long time to get enough data, and I'm not sure the data would ever be good enough to provide the right answer. That would leave people a moral judgment to make.

Time for a Common Understanding

You explore issues in this book that are philosophical, almost philological, in nature. The research community, you point out, doesn't apply words like "involuntary" or "compulsive" with much consistency. Is it time for some common understanding of these ideas?

I hope my book teaches my colleagues in research, as well as the public, that we can talk about things like "voluntary" and "involuntary" behaviour in ways that are testable. We can test whether behaviour is modified by its consequences.

How has genetic theory—the idea that behaviours like drug dependence are determined by biology—influenced this debate?

There was an initial dark period. The initial impulse was to say that nothing that is disordered in our behaviour is voluntary—that everything is a disease. But we're gradually discovering that things which are clearly voluntary, like religious beliefs, have a heritability. So people are going to say, aha, it's not that voluntary behaviours are non-biological and involuntary ones are biological. It's just that they have a different wiring, and the wiring for voluntary ones are more complicated. The neurons are influenced by consequences as well as by preceding biological conditions. Genetics plays a big role in voluntary behaviour, but our brains are wired so that certain activities can be influenced by rewards and punishments.

THREE

Alcoholism Is a Serious Problem for Teens

U.S. Department of Health and Human Services, Office of the Surgeon General

The Office of the Surgeon General oversees the U.S. Public Health Service. The surgeon general is America's chief health educator. In the following viewpoint the author asserts that underage drinking (defined as those who are under the legal drinking age of twenty-one) is a serious problem. The Office of the Surgeon General reports that more young people drink alcohol than smoke cigarettes or use marijuana. A significant number of teens are drinking before the age of thirteen, and studies report that by the time young adults are twenty-one years old, 90 percent have had a drink. Adolescents do not drink as often as adults, according to the author, but when they do drink, they drink more heavily, consuming more drinks at one time than adults do.

Underage alcohol consumption in the United States is a widespread and persistent public health and safety problem that creates serious personal, social, and economic consequences for adolescents, their families, communities, and the Nation as a whole. Alcohol is the drug of choice among America's adolescents, used by more young people than tobacco or illicit

U.S. Department of Health and Human Services, "The Surgeon General's Call to Action to Prevent and Reduce Underage Drinking," www.surgeongeneral.gov/topics/underagedrinking, 2007.

drugs. The prevention and reduction of underage drinking and treatment of underage youth with alcohol use disorders (AUDs) are therefore important public health and safety goals. . . .

The body of research demonstrat[es] the potential negative consequences of underage alcohol use on human maturation, particularly on the brain, which recent [2004] studies show continues to develop into a person's twenties. Although considerable attention has been focused on the serious consequences of underage drinking and driving, accumulating evidence indicates that the range of adverse consequences is much more extensive than that and should also be comprehensively addressed. For example, the highest prevalence of alcohol dependence in the U.S. population is among 18- to 20-year-olds who typically began drinking years earlier. This finding underscores the need to consider problem drinking within a developmental framework. Furthermore, early and, especially, early heavy drinking are associated with increased risk for adverse lifetime alcohol-related consequences. Research also has provided a more complete understanding of how underage drinking is related to factors in the adolescent's environment, cultural issues, and an adolescent's individual characteristics. Taken together, these data demonstrate the compelling need to address alcohol problems early, continuously, and in the context of human development using a systematic approach that spans childhood through adolescence into adulthood.

A Serious Problem

Underage drinking remains a serious problem despite laws against it in all 50 States; decades of Federal, State, Tribal, and local programs aimed at preventing and reducing underage drinking; and efforts by many private entities. Underage drinking is deeply embedded in the American culture, is often viewed as a rite of passage, is frequently facilitated by adults, and has proved stubbornly resistant to change. A new, more comprehensive and developmentally sensitive approach is warranted. . . .

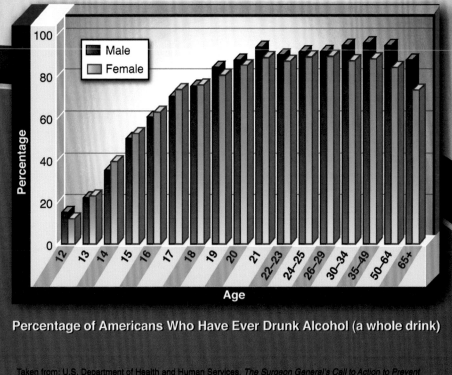

Alcohol Use Increases Dramatically During Adolescence

Percentage of Americans Who Have Ever Drunk Alcohol (a whole drink)

Taken from: U.S. Department of Health and Human Services, *The Surgeon General's Call to Action to Prevent and Reduce Underage Drinking.* Rockville, MD: U.S. Department of Health and Human Services, Office of the Surgeon General, 2007.

Underage Alcohol Use Increases with Age

Alcohol use is an age-related phenomenon. The percentage of the population who have drunk at least one whole drink rises steeply during adolescence until it plateaus at about age 21. By age 15, approximately 50 percent of boys and girls have had a whole drink of alcohol; by age 21, approximately 90 percent have done so.

Alcohol Use Disorders Among the Young

Early alcohol consumption by some young people will result in an alcohol use disorder—that is, they will meet diagnostic criteria for either alcohol abuse or dependence. . . . The highest prevalence of alcohol dependence is among people ages 18–20. In other words, the description these young people provide of their drinking behavior meets the criteria for alcohol dependence set forth in the most recent editions of the *Diagnostic and Statistical Manual of Mental Disorders (DSM)—DSM-IV* and *DSM-IV-TR*.

Even some youth younger than age 18 have an alcohol use disorder. According to data from the 2005 National Survey on Drug Use and Health (NSDUH), 5.5 percent of youth ages 12–17 meet the diagnostic criteria for alcohol abuse or dependence.

The Nature of Underage Drinking

Underage alcohol use is a pervasive problem with serious health and safety consequences for the Nation. The nature and gravity of the problem is best described in terms of the number of children and adolescents who drink, when and how they drink, and the negative consequences that result from drinking.

Alcohol is the most widely used substance of abuse among America's youth. . . . A higher percentage of youth in 8th, 10th, and 12th grades used alcohol in the month prior to being surveyed than used tobacco or marijuana, the illicit drug most commonly used by adolescents.

A *substantial number of young people begin drinking at very young ages*. A number of surveys ask youth about the age at which they first used alcohol. Because the methodology in the various surveys differs, the data are not consistent across them. Nonetheless, they do show that a substantial number of youth begin drinking before the age of 13. For example, data from recent surveys indicate that:

- Approximately 10 percent of 9- to 10-year-olds have started drinking.
- Nearly one-third of youth begin drinking before age 13.
- More than one-tenth of 12- or 13-year-olds and over one-third of 14- or 15-year-olds reported alcohol use (a whole drink) in the past year.
- The peak years of alcohol initiation are 7th and 8th grades.

Heavy Drinkers

Adolescents drink less frequently than adults, but when they do drink, they drink more heavily than adults. When youth between the ages of 12 and 20 consume alcohol, they drink on average about five drinks per occasion about six times a month. . . . This amount of alcohol puts an adolescent drinker in the binge range, which, depending on the study, is defined as "five or more drinks on one occasion" or "five or more drinks in a row for men and four or more drinks in a row for women." By comparison, adult drinkers age 26 and older consume on average two to three drinks per occasion about nine times a month. . . .

Differences in underage alcohol use exist between the sexes and among racial and ethnic groups. Despite differences between the sexes and among racial and ethnic groups, overall rates of

Although teens do not drink as often as adults, they consume a greater amount of alcohol when they do drink.

drinking among most populations of adolescents are high. In multiple surveys, underage males generally report more alcohol use during the past month than underage females. Boys also tend to start drinking at an earlier age than girls, drink more frequently, and are more likely to binge drink. When youth ages 12–20 were asked about how old they were when they started drinking, the average age was 13.90 for boys and 14.36 for girls for those adolescents who reported drinking. Interestingly, the magnitude of the sex-related difference in the frequency of binge drinking varies substantially by age. Further, data from the Monitoring the Future survey show that while the percentages of boys and girls in the 8th and 10th grades who binge drink are similar (10.5 and 10.8, and 22.9 and 20.9, respectively), among 12th graders, boys have a higher prevalence of binge drinking compared to girls (29.8 compared to 22.8).

While the percentage of adolescents of all racial/ethnic subgroups who drink is high, Black or African-American and Asian youth tend to drink the least. . . .

Adverse Consequences of Underage Drinking

The short- and long-term consequences that arise from underage alcohol consumption are astonishing in their range and magnitude, affecting adolescents, the people around them, and society as a whole. Adolescence is a time of life characterized by robust physical health and low incidence of disease, yet overall morbidity and mortality rates increase 200 percent between middle childhood and late adolescence/early adulthood. This dramatic rise is attributable in large part to the increase in risk-taking, sensation-seeking, and erratic behavior that follows the onset of puberty and which contributes to violence, unintentional injuries, risky sexual behavior, homicide, and suicide. Alcohol frequently plays a role in these adverse outcomes and the human tragedies they produce. Among the most prominent adverse consequences of underage alcohol use are those listed below. Underage drinking:

- Is a leading contributor to death from injuries, which are the main cause of death for people under age 21. Annually, about

5,000 people under age 21 die from alcohol-related injuries involving underage drinking. About 1,900 (38 percent) of the 5,000 deaths involve motor vehicle crashes, about 1,600 (32 percent) result from homicides, and about 300 (6 percent) result from suicides.

- Plays a significant role in risky sexual behavior, including unwanted, unintended, and unprotected sexual activity, and sex with multiple partners. Such behavior increases the risk for unplanned pregnancy and for contracting sexually transmitted diseases (STDs), including infection with HIV, the virus that causes AIDS.
- Increases the risk of physical and sexual assault.
- Is associated with academic failure.
- Is associated with illicit drug use.
- Is associated with tobacco use.
- Can cause a range of physical consequences, from hangovers to death from alcohol poisoning.
- Can cause alterations in the structure and function of the developing brain, which continues to mature into the mid- to late twenties, and may have consequences reaching far beyond adolescence.
- Creates secondhand effects that can put others at risk. Loud and unruly behavior, property destruction, unintentional injuries, violence, and even death because of underage alcohol use afflict innocent parties. For example, about 45 percent of people who die in crashes involving a drinking driver under the age of 21 are people other than the driver. Such secondhand effects often strike at random, making underage alcohol use truly everybody's problem.
- In conjunction with pregnancy, may result in fetal alcohol spectrum disorders, including fetal alcohol syndrome, which remains a leading cause of mental retardation.

Further, underage drinking is a risk factor for heavy drinking later in life, and continued heavy use of alcohol leads to increased risk across the lifespan for acute consequences and for medical problems such as cancers of the oral cavity, larynx, pharynx, and esophagus; liver cirrhosis; pancreatitis; and hemorrhagic stroke.

FOUR

The Extent of Teen Alcoholism Is Exaggerated

David J. Hanson

David J. Hanson is professor emeritus of sociology at the State University of New York at Potsdam and has researched alcoholism for more than thirty years. In the following viewpoint Hanson asserts that statistics reporting teen alcohol abuse are distorted, biased, and inaccurate. The proportion of students who drink is at an all-time low, he maintains, nor do teens drink as much as people think they do. However, Hanson adds, the hype and exaggeration of teen drinking contribute to the problem, because teens tend to try to keep up with what they think their peers are doing.

We've all seen the distressing headlines. Case in point—newspapers across the country carried frightening statistics reported by Joe Califano and the Center on Addiction and Substance Abuse (CASA).

On national television programs, Califano reported horror stories of alcohol abuse among college students, associating it with assault, rape, and even murder. A CASA report asserted that:

- "60 percent of college women who have acquired sexually transmitted diseases, including AIDS and genital herpes, were under the influence of alcohol at the time they had intercourse"

David J. Hanson, "Underage Drinking," www.alcoholinformation.org, January 12, 2009. Reproduced by permission of the author.

- "90 percent of all reported campus rapes occur when alcohol is being used by either the assailant or the victim"
- "The number of women who reported drinking to get drunk more than tripled between 1977 and 1993"
- "95 percent of violent crime on campus is alcohol-related"

But relax. These assertions are not supported by the facts. According to an investigative reporter, one of these statistics "appears to have been pulled from thin air," another is based on no evidence whatsoever, another is based on one inadequate survey and is inconsistent with all other surveys, and a fourth is highly suspect at best.

Dispelling a Myth

Even the most improbable of statistics are often repeated by news media as fact and become part of public belief. It is now commonly

Joseph A. (Joe) Califano (pictured) and the Center on Addiction and Substance Abuse released a report to the media indicating that alcohol abuse among college students is associated with rape, assault, and murder.

believed that the average young person will have seen 100,000 beer commercials between the age of two and eighteen.

But just think—sixteen years or about 5,844 days occur between a person's second and eighteenth birthday. To see 100,000 beer commercials in that period, a person would have to see an average of more than seventeen a day!

Common sense alone should have been enough to dispel the myth. But this clearly absurd statistic has been gullibly repeated over and over:

- by the Center for Science in the Public Interest in the *New York Times*
- in *Sports Illustrated*
- in Congressional testimony by Senator Strom Thurmond, the National Council on Alcoholism, and The Center for Children
- by Remove Intoxicated Drivers (RID) on *Sonya Live*
- by former Surgeon General Everett Koop in the *New York Times*
- and in countless newspapers and magazines across the country

This blatantly erroneous statistic has even found its way into textbooks for students and in materials for teachers.

Inflated Statistics

Distorted, biased, or incorrect statistics may attract media attention. They may even influence public policy. But they can't contribute to a reduction of alcohol abuse, which requires accurate information and unbiased interpretation. Therefore, we must be skeptical of surprising, sensationalized statistics.

Typically, inflated statistics are associated with talk of epidemics, threats to our youth, and similar alarmist language. Often they are promoted by groups with laudable sounding names such as the Center for Science in the Public Interest.

But many such groups, which may have underlying social or political agendas, tend to exaggerate the extent and growth of problems in which they have a vested interest and, typically, a proposed solution.

Problems widely seen by the public as being of epidemic proportion justify ever larger budgets, increased staffs, higher salaries, more power, and greater organizational prestige.

And many groups and individuals have a vested interest in exaggerating the extent of drinking problems. They generally include federal, state, and other governmental alcohol agencies; private alcohol agencies; alcohol treatment facilities, therapists, alcohol educators; and often alcohol abusers themselves.

Editors sometimes confess that sensational statistics have much more reader appeal than reports of generally declining problems. Thus, when alcohol statistics are presented by researchers, the media tend to spin stories in a negative light.

A nation-wide survey of students at 168 U.S. colleges and universities found that:

- 98% have never been in trouble with a college administrator because of behavior resulting from drinking too much
- 93% have never received a lower grade because of drinking too much
- 93% have never come to class after having had several drinks
- 90% have never damaged property, pulled a false alarm, or engaged in similar inappropriate behavior because of drinking

College Drinking Rates Are Declining

While headlines typically express alarm over drinking epidemics among collegians, in reality drinking among college students continues to decline as abstaining from alcohol climbs:

- The proportion of college students who abstain from alcohol jumped 58% between 1983 and 1994, according to a series of nation-wide surveys
- A 16% increase in college non-drinkers has been found between the periods of 1989–1991 and 1995–1997 by the federally-funded CORE Institute
- A recent study by Dr. Henry Wechsler of Harvard University found that the proportion of collegiate abstainers in the U.S. jumped nearly 22% in the four years since his earlier study

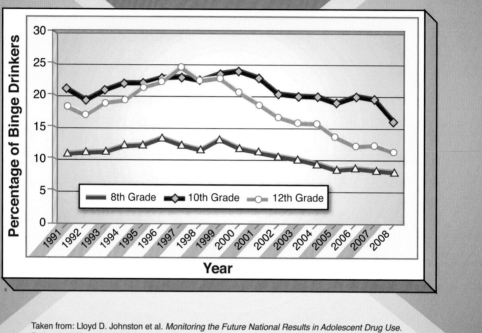

Taken from: Lloyd D. Johnston et al. *Monitoring the Future National Results in Adolescent Drug Use.* Bethesda, MD: National Institute on Drug Abuse, 2008.

- The proportion of non-drinkers among college students in the U.S. recently reached a record-breaking all-time high accoring to statistics collected for the National Institute on Drug Abuse by the Institute for Social Research of the University of Michigan

That means that the proportion of students who drink has dropped to an all-time record-breaking low!

- The proportion of first year college students who drink beer has fallen dramatically and recently reached the lowest level in 30 years, according to national annual surveys by UCLA's Higher Education Research Institute. Similar drops were found for wine and distilled spirits

So-called binge drinking among American college students also continues to decline. For example, the proportion of college students who binge decreased significantly within a recent four-year period, according to the Harvard University study mentioned above. . . .

These findings are consistent with data collected for the National Institute on Drug Abuse by the Institute for Social Research. The ISR found that college "binge" drinking in the U.S. recently reached the lowest level of the entire 17-year period that its surveys have been conducted.

College Students Drink Less than Generally Thought

College students "simply don't drink as much as everyone seems to think they do," according to researchers who used Breathalizers at the University of North Carolina [UNC] at Chapel Hill.

Even on the traditional party nights of Thursday, Friday and Saturday, 66% of the students returned home with absolutely no blood alcohol content; two of every three students had not a trace of alcohol in their systems at the end of party nights.

"I'm not surprised at all by these results," said Rob Foss, manager of Alcohol Studies for the UNC Highway Traffic Safety Center, which conducted the study with funding from the National Highway Traffic Safety Administration and the North Carolina Governor's Highway Safety Program.

"Other Breathalizer studies we have done with drivers and recreational boaters show similar results—less drinking than is generally believed. We have substantial misperceptions about alcohol use in this country."

Similarly, drinking among young people in general continues to decline. For example, the proportion of youths aged 12 through 17 who consumed any alcohol within the previous month has dropped from 50% in 1979 down to 19% in 1998, according to the federal government's National Household Survey on Drug Abuse.

That's down from one of every two youths to fewer than one of every five.

The proportion of both junior and senior high school students who have consumed any alcohol during the year has dropped again for the third year in a row, according to the PRIDE Survey, a nation-wide study of 138,079 students, which is designated by federal law as an official measure of substance use by teen-agers in the U.S.

Within a period of 17 years, there has been a 13% decrease in the proportion of American high school seniors who have ever consumed alcohol and a 24% decrease in the proportion who have ever "binged."

These are very important facts, but you probably haven't seen or heard much, if anything, about them in the mass media.

A Solution

In spite of all the hype and exaggeration, the fact remains that alcohol abuse is still a significant problem among youth that requires our attention. Thus, the question remains: what can we do to reduce alcohol abuse?

Significantly, hype and exaggeration are actually an important part of the problem. A negative spin on drinking statistics has a negative impact on drinking behaviors by contributing to a "reign of error".

When people believe that "everyone is doing it," abusive drinking increases as they try to conform to the imagined behaviors of others.

This is especially true among young people. Perceptions of the drinking behaviors of others strongly influences the actual drinking behavior of students.

The exaggeration of alcohol abuse tends to create a self-fulfilling prophesy. The more young people believe heavy drinking occurs, the more heavily they tend to drink in order to conform.

Research has demonstrated that reducing misperceptions of alcohol abuse is an effective way to reduce actual abuse among adolescents.

Individual students almost always believe that most others on campus drink more heavily than they do and the disparity between the perceived and the actual behaviors tend to be quite large.

By conducting surveys of actual behavior and publicizing the results, the extent of heavy drinking can be quickly and significantly reduced. The most carefully assessed such project demonstrated a 35% reduction in heavy drinking, a 31% reduction in alcohol-related injuries to self, and a 54% reduction in alcohol-related injuries to others.

This approach to reducing alcohol problems is remarkably quick and inexpensive and has proven to be highly effective.

FIVE

Binge Drinking by College Students Is a Serious Problem

Joseph A. Califano

In the following viewpoint Joseph A. Califano argues that the percentage of college students who participate in binge drinking has not declined and that the intensity of heavy drinking has actually increased. In fact, he asserts, the atmosphere on college campuses seems to be one in which administrators and teachers tolerate a culture of binge drinking. It is time, Califano contends, for this culture of tolerance to be changed. Binge and heavy drinking is not a harmless rite of passage but a dangerous activity that threatens the well-being of young adults. Califano is the president and chair of the National Center on Addiction and Substance Abuse (CASA) at Columbia University and the author of *High Society: How Substance Abuse Ravages America and What to Do About It.*

The recent report of The National Center on Addiction and Substance Abuse (CASA) at Columbia University, *Wasting the Best and the Brightest: Substance Abuse at America's Colleges and Universities*, reveals a disturbing ambiance of hedonistic self-indulgence and an alarming public health crisis on college campuses across this nation.

Joseph A. Califano, "Wasting the Best and the Brightest: Alcohol and Drug Abuse on College Campuses," *America,* vol. 196, May 28, 2007. Copyright © 2007 www.americamagazine.org. All rights reserved. Reproduced by permission of America Press. For subscription information, visit www.americamagazine.org.

From 1993, the year of CASA's original assessment of drinking on the nation's campuses, to 2005, the last year for which relevant data are available, there has been no significant reduction in the proportion of students who drink (70 percent vs. 68 percent) and binge drink (a steady 40 percent). Far more troubling, the intensity of excessive drinking and other drug use has risen sharply.

Shocking Results

The shocking results: Half of all full-time college students (3.8 million) binge drink, abuse prescription drugs and/or abuse illegal drugs. Almost one in four of the nation's college students (22.9 percent, some 1.8 million) meet the medical criteria for substance abuse or dependence, two and a half times the proportion (8.5 percent) of those who meet the criteria in the rest of the population.

Rates of dangerous drinking increased from 1993 to 2001, the latest year for which these data are available. Over that period, the proportion of students who:

- binge drink frequently (three or more times in the past two weeks) is up 16 percent;
- drink on 10 or more occasions in the past month is up 25 percent;
- get drunk three or more times in the past month is up 26 percent;
- drink to get drunk is up 21 percent.

And the drug abuse problem among college students goes far beyond alcohol. Since the early 1990's, the proportion of students using marijuana daily has more than doubled. Use of drugs like cocaine and heroin is up 52 percent. Student abuse of prescription opiods, stimulants and tranquillizers has exploded. From 1993 to 2005, the proportion of students who abuse prescription painkillers like Percocet, Vicodin and OxyContin shot up 343 percent to 240,000 students; stimulants like Ritalin and Adderall, 93 percent to 225,000; tranquilizers like Xanax and Valium, 450 percent to 171,000; and sedatives like Nembutal and Seconal, 225 percent to 101,000.

College Students Abuse Alcohol More than the General Population

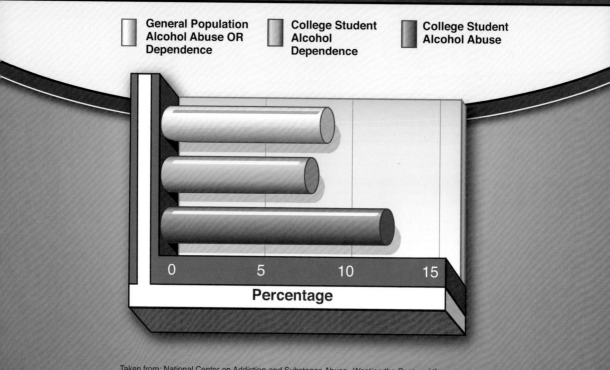

Legend:
- General Population Alcohol Abuse OR Dependence
- College Student Alcohol Dependence
- College Student Alcohol Abuse

Percentage: 0, 5, 10, 15

Taken from: National Center on Addiction and Substance Abuse, *Wasting the Best and the Brightest: Substance Abuse at America's Colleges and Universities*, March, 2007.

Devastating Consequences

This explosion in the intensity of substance abuse among college students carries devastating consequences. Each year:

- more than 1,700 students die from alcohol poisoning and alcohol-related injuries.
- 700,000 students are assaulted by classmates who were drinking.
- almost 100,000 students are victims of alcohol-related sexual assaults and rapes.

Looking at Catholic Institutions

The CASA study, conducted over four years, is the most exhaustive examination ever undertaken of the substance abuse situation among the nation's 7.8 million full-time college students (age 18 to 22). It did not separate out Jesuit college and university students. Sadly, however, there is no reason to believe they are any better than the general population of college students.

Fordham University is ranked New York City's number one school in self-reported campus alcohol violations, with 905 in 2005, more than four times the 194 reported by New York University, which is in second place. (Some of the spread may reflect different reporting methods.) The College of the Holy Cross (my alma mater) has been plagued by a series of tragic incidents over recent years, including accusations of rape by a female student who was drinking heavily (1996), a drunken student killed by a pickup truck (1998), another killed by a train (2000), one killed in a fight between drunken classmates (2002) and a student hospitalized in a booze-fueled rugby team hazing (2002). In Spokane, Wash., Gonzaga University basketball players were picked up on suspicion of possession of drugs (marijuana) in February of this year [2007]. As at most other colleges, students at Holy Cross, Boston College and Georgetown have engaged in alcohol-fueled rowdy conduct and vandalism that has drawn the ire of neighboring residents and local police.

Why Students Drink and Take Drugs

Why do students drink and drug themselves like this? CASA surveyed a nationally representative sample of 2,000 students, who said they did so to relieve stress, relax, have fun, forget their problems and be one of the gang. College women in focus groups said they wanted to keep up with the guys so they went drink for drink with them (though on average one drink has the impact on a woman that two have on a man). These women also said they were under enormous pressure to have sex and they used alcohol as a disinhibitor.

CASA also surveyed some 400 college administrators and interviewed scores of experts in the field, and the findings are disturbing. At many institutions, college presidents, deans, trustees and alumni accept binge drinking and other drug use as a rite of passage. College presidents and trustees are consumed with raising money, building new facilities and recruiting faculty; the substance abuse problem gets low priority. One Ivy League board chair told me that the alumni resisted efforts to reform drinking and related social practices, particularly among fraternities and clubs. (The CASA report found that excessive drinking and other drug abuse was higher among such groups.) Turnover in administrative positions related to student conduct is high, and resources are low. Many Catholic colleges (and several others) have initiated steps, such as education, prevention efforts and AA meetings, to mitigate the problem.

Tolerating a Culture of Substance Abuse

Nevertheless, the CASA report's overall grim conclusion: College presidents, deans and trustees have facilitated or tolerated a college culture of alcohol and drug abuse that is linked to poor student academic performance, depression, anxiety, suicide, property damage, vandalism, fights and a host of medical problems. By failing to become part of the solution, these presidents, deans and trustees have become part of the problem. Their acceptance of the status quo of rampant alcohol and other drug abuse puts the best and the brightest—and the nation's future—in harm's way.

Edward Malloy, C.S.C. [Congregation of the Holy Cross, a Catholic brotherhood of priests and monks], president emeritus of the University of Notre Dame and chair of the CASA advisory commission that supervised the study, says, "College presidents are reluctant to take on issues they feel they cannot change and this growing public health crisis reflects today's society where students are socialized to consider substance abuse a harmless rite of passage and to medicate every ill." These institutions have an obligation to confront the problem of campus substance abuse in order to maintain their academic credibility, to protect the health and

A report by the National Center on Addiction and Substance Abuse found that college officials tolerate a culture of substance abuse by students.

safety of students on their campuses and to preserve their financial resources from liability for injury and death of students as a result of foreseeable harm from the culture of alcohol and drug abuse and addiction. Catholic universities have an added incentive: the recognition that students, like all of us, are made in God's image, with an inherent human dignity that should not be debased by excessive use of alcohol. Catholic college campuses incur a special obligation to discourage an atmosphere of excessive alcohol consumption that facilitates the deadly sin of gluttony.

It is time to take the "high" out of higher education. But school administrators cannot do it alone. As Father Malloy also points out, "To change this culture, college and university presidents will need help from parents, alumni, students, Greek and athletic organizations, and state and federal governments."

Parents bear a significant measure of responsibility. Three-fourths of college drinkers and drug users began drinking and drugging in high school or even earlier. Teen drinking and drug use is a parent problem. Parents who provide the funds for their children in college to purchase alcohol and drugs and party at substance-fueled spring breaks enable the college culture of abuse. If parents cannot say no to children who want to go on such breaks, how can they expect their children to say no to alcohol and marijuana?

What Can Be Done?

Much can be done, and Jesuit colleges can lead the way. They can ban alcohol in dormitories, in most common areas and at campus student parties and college sporting events. They can stop alcohol marketing on campus and at campus athletic events and broadcasts. They should insist that the National College Athletic Association refuse to permit beer advertising during broadcasts of athletic events like the March Madness basketball tournament, which draws a large college audience.

Many students arrange their schedules to have classes only three or four days a week so that their partying can begin on Wednesday or Thursday evening and continue until Monday morning. Colleges have the power to require that full-time students attend classes at least five days a week. Parents who are paying $30,000 to $50,000 a year for room, board and tuition should demand it.

Colleges and universities can engage local authorities to limit the number of bars and retail liquor stores surrounding their campuses. Students should be educated about alcohol abuse, as Georgetown now requires of all freshmen. . . .

The first step is for college administrators, trustees, alumni and parents to accept responsibility for tossing the nation's college students into the high seas of alcohol, tobacco and prescription and illegal drugs that so many college campuses and their surrounding communities have become. Substance abuse–free campuses should be the rule, not the exception. Television broadcasts of college athletic events should not be opportunities for beer merchants to hawk their products to underage undergraduates. Admission to elite clubs and fraternities should not carry the risk of alcohol poisoning. Drunkenness should not mark half-time at college football games. Nor should Ritalin and Adderall abuse be the price of performance.

Most important, college administrators, trustees, alumni and parents should abandon their view that binge drinking is some harmless rite of passage and instead see it for what it truly is: a dangerous game of Russian roulette that threatens our nation's best and brightest.

SIX

The Extent of "Binge Drinking" on Campus Is Not Increasing

Robert J. Chapman

Robert J. Chapman is a clinical associate professor of behavioral health counseling at Drexel University in Philadelphia. In the following viewpoint Chapman contends that while a large percentage of college students participate in high-risk drinking, the numbers are not as alarming as they first appear to be. College freshmen and sophomores typically are the heaviest drinkers in college. But as these students mature, Chapman reports, they are no longer the heavy drinkers they were in their first and second years of college. However, he asserts, as these students mature and graduate, they are replaced by new freshmen and sophomores, who begin the maturation process anew. This cyclical process explains why the percentage of college students who are heavy drinkers remains static.

High-risk drinking is a phenomenon that has been the focus of attention in higher education for 10 years since the first Harvard School of Public Health "College Alcohol Survey" (CAS) results were published in 1994. Yet prior to 1994, this phenomenon was frequently observed and if not empirically understood, at least anecdotally documented by anyone that has attended a college, worked in higher ed or owned property contiguous to a collegiate campus.[1]

A Rite of Passage

Students view collegiate drinking as a phenomenon so ubiquitous as to be considered a developmental "rite of passage." "Older" adults remember their experiences with alcohol in college fondly and find it difficult to find fault with the consumption of alcohol by any aged collegian of today, all the time voicing increasing concern for student consumption of "other drugs." It would seem that in the U.S. we have settled into something of a "co-dependent" relationship with collegiate drinking—we disapprove of its impact on student behavior but all but celebrate its contribution to a meaningful college experience. This is a love-hate relationship and we have gone to great lengths in recent years to address the "problem of binge drinking" while defending a collegian's right to "drink responsibly."

There have been fluctuations in the numbers of students engaging in dangerous drinking thanks in part to innovative programming like social norms campaigns and brief motivational interviews with high-risk drinkers as well as an increasing awareness of the role that environmental and ecological strategies can play in shaping a campus culture. Yet the rates of student drinking persist—81% of collegians nationally drink according to the most recent Harvard CAS studies, and this is as high as 90+% in some areas of the country—whereas about 66% of adults nationally report drinking. The rates of high-risk or dangerous drinking—terms much more suited to this phenomenon than "binge-drinking"—show no signs of yielding with about 44% of contemporary collegians reporting that they drank in a high-risk fashion (5+ drinks in an outing) in the 2 weeks prior to being surveyed in these same Harvard CAS samples.

Although this could lead one to hypothesize that contemporary collegians are, "Going to Hell in a booze soaked hand basket,"

1. See also: http://robertchapman.net/essays.htm.

Little Change in College Drinking Rates

Drinking trends among college students have not changed much over the years. Studies show that college students maintain a heavy rate of binge drinking (five or more drinks in one sitting) that has changed little over the years. The binge rate of 41.1 percent in 2007 is nearly identical to the binge rate of 41.4 percent in 1992.

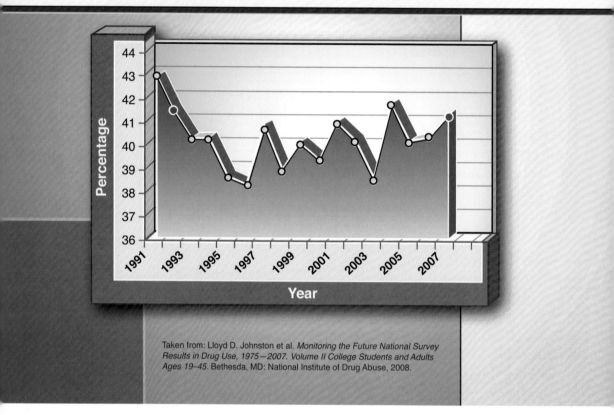

Taken from: Lloyd D. Johnston et al. *Monitoring the Future National Survey Results in Drug Use, 1975–2007. Volume II College Students and Adults Ages 19–45.* Bethesda, MD: National Institute of Drug Abuse, 2008.

there may be more to this story than is apparent at first glance. The "rest of the story," as the famed newscaster Paul Harvey says in his well-known radio broadcasts, may hold something of significance for us Student Affairs professionals as we consider how to "better" address this stubborn, if not intractable [difficult to manage] problem of high-risk collegiate drinking.

An Examination of Who Is Drinking

Let's take another look at those Harvard CAS samples that suggest so many contemporary collegians drink and that a sizeable minority of them do so in a high-risk fashion. There is no doubt that these numbers are alarming, but it is incumbent upon the Student Affairs professional to look at these data a little closer and note "which" collegians are doing the drinking. Of the high-risk drinkers on a given campus, what proportion of them are first or second-year students? We know that the majority—some estimates run as high as 75%—of entering first-year students bring their high school drinking habits and preferences with them. With the newly acquired freedom that accompanies collegiate life, these high school preferences and

First- and second-year college students are at highest risk for alcohol abuse, but by their junior year—having recognized the connection between poor grades and drinking—their alcohol use may decline.

practices flourish if not expand. The result is that first and second year students are among the highest-risk drinkers in college. As they realize the correlation, however, between drinking a belly fully of beer on a Friday night and their grades at the end of the semester—not to mention the preponderance of "drunk calls" made on the omnipresent cell phone with speed dial to former significant others at 2 AM or apologies that have to be extended for vomit deposited on the desk in a friend's dorm room—students begin to moderate their behavior in general and drinking specifically. This is so widely recognized as to have been named the "maturing out phenomenon" and we see it with virtually every student that enters college. Whether this results from experience or is a part of a natural maturational process is irrelevant to this essay's intent. Suffice it to say that students change their attitudes, values and belief—and consequently their behaviors—as they progress through the semesters in their collegiate experience. . . .

If a sizeable portion of the high-risk drinkers in a sample drawn from a collegiate population come from 1st and 2nd-year students, this is important for Student Affairs professionals to recognize, and many do. Special programming that targets these students has been successful in hastening the maturing out phenomenon. But the point remains that each year these more mature students graduate and are replaced by entering 1st-year students who bring their high-school attitudes, values and beliefs with them to the newfound freedom of collegiate life, and there in lies the rub. Like St. Augustine trying to empty the sea with a shell, Student Affairs professionals as well as senior collegiate administrators are left each year with a cohort of new students whose movement through the maturing out process must once again begin in earnest, shepherded by Student Affairs professionals, other staff and faculty. Each year a new wave of students unfamiliar with college and its demands arrives on campus already habituated to a high-risk pattern of socializing, and thus the process begins anew . . . just like [actor] Bill Murray's experience in [the film] "Groundhog Day."

Little Is Going to Change

Although unaware of any research that tests my "Groundhog Day" hypothesis, its logic alone suggests that its consideration may shed some light on why the alcohol-related numbers on collegiate drinking surveys remain so static. And if this hypothesis is born out, it suggests that until and unless colleges and universities begin to partner more effectively with high schools in general and their "feeder schools" specifically, little is going to change.

The Good News

The good news is that efforts to partner with high schools—and even earlier—have already begun. Wesley Perkins and David Craig at Hobart-William Smith College in N.Y. are conducting groundbreaking work in the area of addressing high school student misperceptions about the social norms in their peer group. In addition, other schools like La Salle University in Philadelphia have established consortia to open the lines of communication with their feeder schools and begin the process of effective prevention programming BEFORE its future students ever arrive on campus.

We have come a long way in recent years regarding the quest to address high-risk collegiate drinking. The issue is appropriately on the "short list" of every college senior administrator across the country. Innovative programs steeped in awareness of how environmental management strategies and the use of the social ecology model are changing the way colleges and universities address these problems "as we speak."

As Dickens wrote in his opening paragraph to *A Tale of Two Cities*, "It was the best of times. It was the worst of times," we have new tools to use but much work to do. However, as another, more contemporary sage, [newspaper columnist] Art Buchwald, mused, "Whether it's the best of times or the worst of times, it's the only time we've got."

SEVEN

There Is a Genetic Predisposition to Alcoholism

John Nurnberger, interviewed by Patrick Perry

Patrick Perry is a writer for *The Saturday Evening Post*. John Nurnberger, director of the Institute of Psychiatric Research at Indiana University School of Medicine, has researched the genetics of alcoholism for decades. In the following viewpoint Nurnberger discusses a study in which researchers performed brain-wave studies and analyzed the DNA of more than twelve thousand people who had a relative diagnosed with alcohol dependence. Nurnberger maintains that researchers found that people with variants of specific genes often developed problems with alcohol or started drinking earlier than those who did not have the variant. Nurnberger asserts that a person's vulnerability to alcohol dependence is 50 percent related to his or her genes. He reports that other studies have found that children of alcoholics who are adopted and raised by non-drinking parents are more likely to have problems with alcohol due to their genes.

We've come a long way in understanding the cunning, baffling disease known as alcoholism, and 12-step programs have helped millions of men and women recover.

Patrick Perry and John Nurnberger, "Unraveling the Genetics of Alcoholism: Recent Discoveries Are Paving the Way to Improved Detection, Prevention, and Treatment Strategies for Alcoholism and Other Forms of Substance Abuse," *Saturday Evening Post*, vol. 279, September/October 2007. © 2007 Saturday Evening Post Society. Reproduced by permission.

Historically, alcoholic behavior was blamed on a character flaw or weakness of will. After all, couldn't people stop drinking if they really wanted to? While the stigma surrounding alcoholism continues, scientists have gained considerably more insight into how genes and environment interact to affect vulnerability to alcoholism—knowledge that is key to reducing the disease's exacting toll on individuals, families, and society.

As more genes are linked to the development of alcohol dependence and substance abuse, the findings will prove useful in developing tools for better gauging individual risk for the disease and identifying those with alcohol problems. Emerging genetic and environmental insights have also paved the way to the discovery of new therapies targeting specific genes or treatments tailored to individual backgrounds.

The [*Saturday Evening*] *Post* spoke with John Nurnberger, M.D., Ph.D., director of the Institute of Psychiatric Research at Indiana University School of Medicine and a leading researcher on the genetics of alcoholism for decades.

A Large-Scale Study

Patrick Perry: *Could you tell us about your work with the Collaborative Study on the Genetics of Alcoholism (COGA), and how alcoholics and family members have helped?*

Dr. [John] Nurnburger: . . . For the past 18 years, we have collaborated to identify families through persons diagnosed with alcohol dependence located at treatment facilities. Once we identified the individual, we would obtain permission to contact relatives of the person to discuss diagnoses in the extended family. We would then perform a brain wave study and take blood for DNA analysis.

In this way COGA established a huge database of information on 12,000 persons across the country. We organized the information to illuminate conditions that surfaced in families with a vulnerability to alcohol dependence and also to uncover the relationship of the brain electrical activity and DNA markers to those conditions.

Findings from the Study

Our group published a number of reports on findings from this sample over the years. We found that a variety of conditions go along with alcohol dependence in families, including dependence on various drugs—marijuana, opiates, tobacco, stimulants, and sedatives. We also noted that a constellation of anxiety and depressive disorders tend to cluster with alcohol problems.

In addition, we observed particular electrical activity signatures in the brain and specific single genes, such as those coding for GABRA2 (a receptor for a transmitter chemical that inhibits other signals), ADH4 (which breaks down alcohol in the body), and CHRM2 (another brain transmitter receptor).

COGA remains very active in various ways: one, we're looking for additional genes in the families we have been studying; and two, we identified adolescents in these families and are following them over time. This is a special high-risk population, and we're trying to determine risk and protective factors that impact young people growing up in families with multiple alcohol-dependent relatives. We are now at a point where some young people in the group are experiencing problems with alcohol but others are not, providing insights into how genes interact with family experience.

In doing the adolescent study, one interesting finding is that the pattern related to specific genes is unexpected. For example, in young people with genetic variations in the GABRA2 neurotransmitter receptor gene, we expected to see alcohol problems and we didn't. Instead, we observed conduct disorder. While you have to study adults to see the alcohol problem, in kids it's more behavior problems. When you look at persons who have the ADH4 gene variant, they begin drinking very early. When you observe persons with the CHRM2 gene variant, they experience depression and anxiety at greater rates as children. Later, they may develop alcohol problems. . . .

Are we at a point where we tailor treatment to best address an individual's specific genetic profile?

Not yet. There are not too many instances in which a genetic test would be of particular value as part of an individual's medical exam for alcohol dependence. But things may change rapidly in the next few years.

Genetics Is Not Destiny

In your . . . article in Scientific American *you wrote, "Genetics is never destiny." What can physicians and members of high-risk families do with the emerging information about vulnerability to alcoholism or substance abuse?*

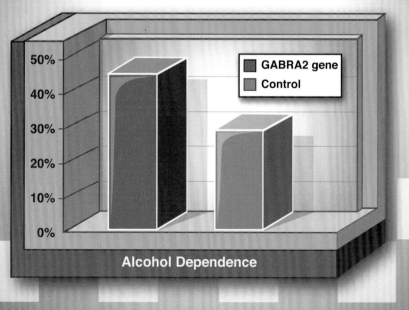

The GABRA2 Gene Is Associated with Alcohol Dependence

Studies have shown an association between the GABRA2 gene (gamma-aminobutyric acid type A receptor) and alcohol dependence. A German study examined 257 people with alcohol dependence and 88 healthy controls. Researchers studied whether variations in the GABRA2 gene were associated with alcohol dependence, taking into consideration whether those who were alcohol dependent had alcohol withdrawal seizures, delirium tremens, and anti-social personality disorder. The study found that the GABRA2 alleles were significantly more common in patients who were dependent on alcohol than in the controls.

Taken from: C. Fehr et al. "Confirmation of Association of the GABRA2 Gene with Alcohol Dependence by Subtype-Specific Analysis," *Psychiatric Genetics*, 2006.

We are trying to understand the biochemical pathways to vulnerability so that new treatments can be designed. Just because a condition is related to genetics doesn't mean it can't be treated or altered. Genetic vulnerabilities are simply that—vulnerabilities. While you can't alter the DNA code you're born with, you can alter the way the genes are expressed and how your body makes proteins from that DNA. In fact, medications can change gene expression, as can exercise. In effect, you can help turn off or turn on various genes by what you do, what medications you take, and the foods that you eat. It's very important for people to realize that, because there is a prominent notion that "you've got a gene for this or that, therefore the condition is inevitable." That's not at all the case.

We have to think differently about how genes actually work. In the body, gene expression is a very malleable process. We are trying to understand what the specific genes are that relate to alcohol dependence and how they work. We know some of them already, such as the GABRA2, the ADH4, and the CHRM2 that I mentioned.

Other Addictions

Will your research findings apply to other addictions, such as smoking?

Yes. There is a genetic profile for tobacco dependence, as well as for alcohol dependence. The two conditions overlap quite a bit. Some of the overlap relates to a general predilection to addiction, and some has to do with specific aspects of nicotine or alcohol. We're beginning to understand the interaction. New evidence regarding the treatment response for people with tobacco dependence is very interesting with regard to the ability of genetic tests to predict treatment response to bupropion (Wellbutrin), one of the agents used to help people stop smoking. It may be that bupropion treatment is very good for persons with certain gene variants, while another treatment modality will help persons with other gene variants.

In the course of meeting these families, has increased self-awareness of genetic risk helped individuals make more informed choices?

In our clinic, the information has helped persons with bipolar illness; that's where I have the greatest exposure to individuals over time. The knowledge makes a difference in the way people think about themselves and their vulnerabilities. If they know that they are vulnerable to a certain substance, they may not stay away from it initially. Over time and with experience, they learn. . . .

Alcohol Dependence and Genetics

What percentage of vulnerability to alcohol dependence is related to genetics?

For alcohol dependence, about 50 percent is related to genetic factors and the other half to environmental factors, such as availability of alcohol and cultural factors. In comparison, the heritability of bipolar illness is about 80 percent, while the heritability of major depression is about 60 percent. Alcohol dependence is less heritable, but still substantially influenced by genetics. In general, there is rarely a situation where there's a 100 percent chance that someone is going to inherit the disorder, except in a single-gene condition, such as Huntington's disease. Most of the diseases we study and treat are conditions of complex inheritance, where there is an increased or a decreased risk. . . .

Alcoholism and Adoption

In studies of children of alcoholics who were adopted by nondrinking families, does alcohol tend to emerge less often, harking back to the role of the environment?

While we haven't done adoption studies in Indiana, studies have been done, primarily in Scandinavian countries that have central records of adoption and psychiatric hospitalization that investigators can access. It does appear that the chance for alcohol dependence is greater in adopted-away children of alcoholics,

Some studies have shown that children of alcoholics are more genetically predisposed to develop an alcohol problem—even if they have been reared by an adoptive family who does not abuse alcohol.

even if they are not brought up in families with the alcoholic person. One still faces increased risk from the genes.

What is your overall hope by identifying genetic influences on vulnerability?

Identifying genetic influences helps us on the road to self-knowledge and leads to strategies for optimal health and a productive life. The field is opening up in front of us. We will witness very real changes in the next couple of decades.

EIGHT

Nurture Can Overcome Genetic Predisposition to Alcoholism

National Institutes of Health

> The National Institutes of Health (NIH) is the primary federal agency responsible for conducting and support-ing medical research. The following viewpoint is a press release from the NIH about a study in Georgia which found that adolescents in a program that worked with parents to help their children avoid substance abuse were less likely to engage in risky behaviors than a control group that did not receive the parenting help. The NIH reports that further analysis showed that the adolescents in the control group who had a genetic variation that is associated with impulsivity, low self-control, binge drink-ing, and substance abuse were more than twice as likely to participate in risky behaviors than their peers with the genetic variation who were in the family program.

A family-based prevention program designed to help adoles-cents avoid substance use and other risky behavior proved especially effective for a group of young teens with a genetic risk factor contributing toward such behavior, according to a new [2009] study by researchers at the University of Georgia. The National Institute on Alcohol Abuse and Alcoholism (NIAAA) and the National Institute on Drug Abuse (NIDA), components

National Institutes of Health, "Prevention Program Helps Teens Override a Gene Linked to Risky Behavior," www.nih.gov/news/health/may2009/niaaa-15.htm, May 15, 2009.

of the National Institutes of Health, supported the study, which appears in the May/June [2009] issue of *Child Development*.

A Long-Term Prevention Program

For two-and-a-half years, investigators monitored the progress of 11-year-olds enrolled in a family-centered prevention program called Strong African American Families (SAAF), and a comparison group. A DNA analysis showed some youths carried the short allele form of 5-HTTLPR. This fairly common genetic variation, found in over 40 percent of people, is known from previous studies to be associated with impulsivity, low self-control, binge drinking, and substance use.

A 2009 study found that traits such as impulsivity, low self-control, substance abuse, and binge drinking are associated with a fairly common gene variation.

The researchers found that adolescents with this gene who participated in the SAAF program were no more likely than their counterparts without the gene to have engaged in drinking, marijuana smoking, and sexual activity. Moreover, youths with the gene in the comparison group were twice as likely to have engaged in these risky behaviors as those in the prevention group.

"The findings underscore that 'nurture' can influence 'nature' during adolescence, a pivotal time when delaying the start of alcohol consumption and other risky behaviors can have a significant impact on healthy child development," says NIAAA Acting Director Kenneth R. Warren, Ph.D. "This study is one of the first to combine prevention research with a gene-environment study design."

"This study is an excellent example of how we can target prevention interventions based on a person's genetic make-up to reduce their substance abuse risk," says NIDA Director Nora Volkow, M.D.

The SAAF Study

The research team recruited 641 families in rural Georgia with similar demographic characteristics. They were divided randomly into two groups: 291 were assigned to a control group that received three mailings of health-related information, and 350 were assigned to the SAAF program, in which parents and children participated in seven consecutive weeks of two-hour prevention sessions. The parents learned about effective caregiving strategies that included monitoring, emotional support, family communication, and handling racial discrimination, which can contribute to substance abuse. The children were taught how to set and attain positive goals, deal with peer pressure and stress, and avoid risky activities.

Researchers conducted home visits with the families when the children were ages 11, 12, and 14 and collected data on parent-child relationships, peer relationships, youth goals for the future, and youth risk behavior. Two years later, the scientists collected DNA from saliva samples provided by the adolescents

Program Deterring Youth Alcohol Use Has Other Positive Effects

A University of Georgia program designed to reduce alcohol use and other risky behaviors among African American youth also reduces the likelihood of other problematic behaviors up to two years later. The Strong African American Families (SAAF) program consists of seven weekly meetings in which parents and pre-adolescent youth participate in activities, games, and specially designed videos to strengthen family relationships. Parents learn how to monitor and communicate with their children, and the youths learn how to set goals and manage peer pressure. Other benefits of the program include:

- **Alcohol use was reduced by 28 percent two years following intervention and 25 percent six years later.**

- Sexual behavior and marijuana use decreased.

- **Caregiver depression was reduced.**

- The likelihood of youth with low self-control engaging in conduct problems was decreased by 74 percent two years later.

Taken from: University of Georgia, "Program Deterring Youth Alcohol Use Has Positive Side Effects," December 22, 2008.

to determine whether they carried the short allele of 5HTTLPR. The results confirmed that the adolescents carrying this risk gene who were in the control group engaged in risky behaviors at a rate double that of their peers in the SAAF program.

"We found that the prevention program proved especially beneficial for children with a genetic risk factor tied to risky behaviors," says the lead author, Gene H. Brody, Ph.D., Regents Professor and Director of the Center for Family Research at the University of Georgia. "The results emphasize the important role of parents, caregivers, and family-centered prevention programs in promoting healthy development during adolescence, especially when children have a biological makeup that may pose a challenge."

Dr. Brody also notes that much of the protective influence of SAAF results from enhancing parenting practices. "The ability of effective parenting to override genetic predispositions to risky behaviors demonstrates the capacity of family-centered prevention programs to benefit developing adolescents," he says. The study team, which included researchers from the University of Iowa and Vanderbilt University, concluded that the results validate the use of randomized, controlled prevention trials to test hypotheses about the ways in which genes and environments interact.

NINE

Alcoholics Have a Natural Tolerance for Alcohol

Jim Atkinson

Jim Atkinson, a reporter for *The New York Times*, is an alcoholic who has written about drinking for a Weblog for the *Times*. In the following viewpoint Atkinson theorizes that people with a high tolerance for alcohol are more likely to become alcoholics. Because of their high tolerance, they are able to drink more without realizing how drunk they are. These repeated episodes of overdrinking change their brain chemistry, which is one of the effects of alcoholism.

I had my last drink nearly 16 years ago, so you'd think I would have assimilated pretty much every bit of unpleasantness associated with clean and sober life in a society that remains thoroughly sodden with alcohol. But I still can't quite handle the holidays.

The Holiday Stress

It's not that I'm driven to drink; just to a certain uncomfortable distraction that doesn't leave until the holiday season thankfully does. And it's not just that the holidays seem to have been invent-

ed for the express purpose of promoting—no, necessitating—
irresponsible alcoholic consumption.

There's something in the alone-in-the-crowdness of the holiday party circuit, the forced pleasantries and laughter, the charge
to be friendly and engaging—but only in a trivial and superficial
way—that is very much like the existential condition of the alcoholic psyche. So the holidays not only remind me of drink; they
remind me of how it felt to be a drunk.

In fact, I have frequently been overheard to explain to the sort
of person who still finds it good sport to ask me how I came to be
addicted to alcohol and what it's like now to be stone cold sober,
"You know how you feel at Christmas at the umpteenth family
gathering or company cocktail party. You really *need* that drink,
right? That's the way I used to feel *all the time*."

And as with one's first adolescent love, a certain euphoric recall
about the drinking life remains lodged in the psyche of any drunk
no matter how many years he has remained sober. Even after 16
years, especially at holiday time, a tiny voice still occasionally
visits, asking, "Why can't you just have one?"

The Alcoholic Psyche

Addiction scientists have puzzled over what distinguishes the
alcoholic psyche from the "normal" one, or even, the mentally
ill one. While some association between abusive drinking and
both bipolar disorder and depression has been found, your garden-
variety drunk does not go on manic flights of fancy or hear voices
or hallucinate; he isn't even all that prone to clinical depression.
The best I can say from personal experience is that we all tend to
be afflicted by a low-grade dysphoria, a sort of constant melan-
choly that causes feelings of unease, isolation and dissatisfaction
with life—an "inexplicable ache," I once heard it called.

But is this nature or nurture? I personally have come to believe
in a construction proposed by Dr. Mark Willenbring, director of
the division of treatment and recovery research at the National
Institute on Alcohol Abuse and Alcoholism, which says it's both.
Willenbring argues that the main thing that alcoholics share is

What Are the Symptoms of Alcoholism?

Alcoholism and alcohol abuse can be diagnosed by doctors when a patient's drinking causes distress or harm. See if you recognize any of these symptoms in yourself. In the past year, have you (check below):

- ☐ had times when you ended up drinking more, or longer, than you intended?

- ☐ more than once wanted to cut down or stop drinking, or tried to, but couldn't?

- ☐ more than once gotten into situations while or after drinking that increased your chances of getting hurt, such as driving, swimming, using machinery, walking in a dangerous area, or having unsafe sex?

- ☐ had to drink much more than you once did to get the effect you want? Or found that your usual number of drinks had much less effect than before?

- ☐ continued to drink even though it was making you feel depressed or anxious or adding to another health problem? Or after having a memory blackout?

- ☐ spent a lot of time drinking? Or being sick or getting over other aftereffects?

- ☐ continued to drink even though it was causing trouble with your family or friends?

- ☐ found that drinking—or being sick from drinking—often interfered with taking care of your home or family? Or caused job troubles? Or school problems?

- ☐ given up or cut back on activities that were important or interesting to you, or gave you pleasure, in order to drink?

- ☐ more than once gotten arrested, been held at a police station, or had other legal problems because of your drinking?

- ☐ found that when the effects of alcohol were wearing off, you had withdrawal symptoms, such as trouble sleeping, shakiness, restlessness, nausea, sweating, a racing heart, or a seizure? Or sensed things that were not there?

a natural tolerance for alcohol, which leads them to overindulge without knowing it. Repeated overindulgence, in turn, changes their brain chemistry and literally creates the inexplicable ache by altering the activity of two systems: the brain's "reward system," which sends the message that drinking feels good; and the excitatory and stress response systems, which become "recruited" and, over time, produce an elevated anxiety when one is without alcohol in his system.

A Tolerance for Alcohol

This would pretty much track my personal experience. It always took more to get me drunk, and the irony is, I always thought that was a good thing. Particularly during my 20's, when everyone was drinking pretty heavily, I could still drink my friends under the table and inspire compliments from them for it. On one occasion, a bunch of us gathered at a friend's apartment to watch a Dallas Cowboys football game. The drinking was heavy and mixed— from beer to scotch and back again, as I recall. At one point late in the fourth quarter, I noticed that *all* of my buddies had passed out—leaving only me to watch the Cowboys lose while I happily mixed a nightcap.

My natural tolerance is probably why, in the mid-80's I was able to score a nice book contract to write "The View from Nowhere," a fairly shameless nationwide pub crawl in search of America's best hard drinking bars. My appearance on the "Today Show" in 1987 to hype the book was proof positive, as it were, that this particular metabolic capability was a boon to my writing career, and would make me less, not more, prone to developing a drinking problem.

But over time, drinking twice as much just to "get there" and feeling proud that I was still not slurring my words took its toll. Without realizing it, I crossed over from mere psychological addiction (a problematic, but self-manageable condition) to physical addiction, which involves blackouts and dangerous withdrawal symptoms, and for which medical intervention is necessary.

It was the under-the-radar aspect of my addiction that still amazes me. I know this is a sensation shared by other drunks

According to the author, because of their high tolerance for alcohol, many alcoholics can drink large quantities of alcohol without displaying the typical characteristics of drunkenness.

because every time I enter an Alcoholics Anonymous room, I am struck not by the expressions of guilt or defiance or even boredom that I see. I am struck by a more or less uniform look of cosmic bafflement on the faces of my fellow addicts. *How in the world did this happen?*

A Self-Destructive Affair

If you are among the 80 percent of people who drink "normally," think of your relationship to booze as a minor friendship that strikes up at certain times of the week, or even the year. Think of the drunk's as a torrid, reckless and self-destructive affair. Whiskey she is a bad lover, and all that. It is a decidedly adolescent affair, a kind of puppy love that overtakes all good judgment and reason. In that sense, I've come to understand that, if compulsive drinking is about different genes, it also about a certain arrested development that can't be liberated until the addict takes the cure.

So how about that one holiday drink? Should I?

Moderate Drinking

The current drift of public thinking about alcohol dependence suggests that perhaps I could. Among the many victims of the Internet age is the notion that anybody with a drinking problem is an alcoholic, period, and needs to go to treatment for 28 days and A.A. thereafter. Today, largely because of the exchanges of addicts on line, there is a growing lobby to treat at least some problem drinkers with more lenience. Google the term "moderate drinking" and you'll find a fistful of Web-based organizations like Drink/Link and Moderation Management that preach a slightly more liberal message than AA: that a lot of drinkers who overindulge can be taught to moderate their drinking.

So if I were sobering up today, I suppose I would have more options than I did 16 years ago. But I don't think that my common sense decisions would be any different. I now know that I'm not totally incorrigible when it comes to the sauce. But I also know that my drinking was more than a bad habit or a passing fancy.

Not Worth the Risk

If I decided to take a drink at a party, I might be able to tough it out for that night, but I know that the next day, another drink would be someplace in my mind. That someplace might be a manageable place, but would it be worth the considerable hassle of having to think twice every time I took a sip?

Besides, my newly wired brain doesn't really have the interest to try. I've worked too hard at this, learned too much, have too much pride in accomplishing something that a lot of folks with this problem don't—a solid sobriety that has lasted at least as long as my addiction did—to risk a relapse.

But what to do about the holidays? I rather like the view of radio talk show host Don Imus, himself a recovering alcoholic who has been sober 20 years. When the subject of parties came up on his radio show a few years back, Imus noted that he was invited to many but went to very few, for one simple reason: "I don't drink."

This seemed to me to be one of the more sensible things ever said about parties or alcoholism. So as the holiday season gets underway, I try to look at it this way. No one really wants to go to all those parties. I'm one of the lucky ones who has an excuse to beg off.

TEN

A Natural Tolerance for Alcohol Is Not What Causes Alcoholism

Stanton Peele

> Stanton Peele is a social and clinical psychologist who
> has written extensively about alcoholism. In the following
> viewpoint he refutes the assertion by Jim Atkinson that
> a person's high tolerance for alcohol leads to alcoholism.
> According to Peele, research does not support this view,
> and he cites the example of Native Americans who tend
> to have a very low tolerance for alcohol and yet have high
> rates of alcoholism.

The [*New York*] *Times* runs a regular blog called *Proof* which
engages discussions of the good and bad, the pleasure and
danger, of alcohol. The current post [December 8, 2008] is by
Jim Atkinson, who wrote a book about drinking, then after years
(decades) discovered he was an alcoholic who needed to go to
AA and abstain to recover. He figures he had a natural tolerance
for alcohol that led him to drink so much for such a long period
that he couldn't avoid being an alcoholic. This explanation of
his addiction doesn't make sense.

One Version of Reality

Here's Atkinson's (and the NIAAA's [National Institute on
Alcohol Abuse and Alcoholism]) version of reality:

I personally have come to believe in a construction proposed by Dr. Mark Willenbring, director of the division of treatment and recovery research at the National Institute on Alcohol Abuse and Alcoholism, which . . . argues that the main thing that alcoholics share is a natural tolerance for alcohol, which leads them to overindulge without knowing it. Repeated overindulgence, in turn, changes their brain chemistry. . . .

What if you had a great tolerance for alcohol, so that you could drink more than most people for many years? Would that be how you spent your time? What would motivate you to do so? Atkinson describes his social life:

. . . . during my 20's, when everyone was drinking pretty heavily, I could still drink my friends under the table and inspire compliments from them for it. On one occasion, a bunch of us gathered at a friend's apartment to watch a Dallas Cowboys football game. The drinking was heavy and mixed—from beer to scotch and back again, as I recall. At one point late in the fourth quarter, I noticed that all of my buddies had passed out—leaving only me to watch the Cowboys lose while I happily mixed a nightcap.

An Unhealthy Way to Spend Time

Do you—or did you—attend many social functions where everyone passed out? If you did, do you think a friend or lover might have suggested that you re-evaluate how you spent your time, and perhaps diversify your interests? Maybe go to some museums, or movies, or lectures. But Atkinson didn't alter his behavior after his 20's. Instead, "My natural tolerance is probably why, in the mid-80's I was able to score a nice book contract to write *The View from Nowhere*, a fairly shameless nationwide pub crawl in search of America's best hard drinking bars." Does Atkinson's use of "shameless" indicate that perhaps he had nagging misgivings about his behavior? But he doesn't say so here.

Estimating Blood Alcohol Content (BAC) per Drink for Men and Women

Blood alcohol content (BAC) measures the concentration of alcohol in the blood. The legal limit of intoxication is .08 percent. While men and women absorb alcohol at different rates, it is generally accepted that one standard drink (1.5 ounces of liquor, 5 ounces of wine, or 12 ounces of beer) raises the BAC from .02 to .05 percent. Most first-time drinkers would be unconscious at .20 percent, and BAC of .35 and .40 percent is potentially fatal.

Body Weight in Pounds—Women/Men

Drinks per Hour	90	100	120	140	160	180	200	220	240
1	.05/-	.05/.03	.04/.03	.03/.02	.03/.02	.03/.02	.02/.02	.02/.02	-/.02
2	.10/-	.09/.08	.08/.06	.07/.05	.06/.05	.05/.04	.05/.04	.04/.03	-/.03
3	.15/-	.14/.11	.11/.08	.10/.07	.09/.06	.08/.06	.07/.05	.06/.05	-./05
4	.20/-	.18/.15	.15/.12	.13/.11	.11/.09	.10/.08	.09/.08	.08/.07	-/.06
5	.25/-	.23/.19	.19/.16	.16/.13	.14/.12	.13/.11	.11/.09	.10/.09	-/.08
6	.30/-	.27/.23	.23/.19	.19/.16	.17/.14	.15/.13	.14/.11	.12/.10	-/.09
7	.35/-	.32/.26	.27/.22	.23/.19	.20/.16	.18/.15	.16/.13	.14/.12	-/.11
8	.40/-	.36/.30	.30/.25	.26/.21	.23/.19	.20/.17	.18/.15	.17/.14	-/.13
9	.45/-	.41/.34	.34/.28	.29/.24	.26/.21	.23/.19	.20/.17	.19/.15	-/.14
10	.51/-	.45/.38	.38/.31	.32/.27	.28/.23	.25/.21	.23/.19	.21/.17	-/.16

Blood Alcohol Content

Taken from: University of Louisiana. www.louisiana.edu/Student/Counseling/SLIDDE/BAC_chart.pdf.

Would you feel comfortable spending night after night in hard-drinking bars? I know many people who wouldn't, including thankfully my three children. My youngest is a college junior in New York City who has many opportunities—and venues—for partying but who seems to prefer to spend her time in other ways. I like to think values like those favoring thinking and positive activity, accomplishing school goals and not wasting her parents' money and others she was taught helped to innoculate her.

Atkinson never discusses such values. He seems to lack that level of discourse, or psychological insight. Despite his ability to gorge great quantities of alcohol, he seems not to have reflected over the decades of his drinking and drunkenness about why he drank so much, what it meant about his life, whether there were better ways to live, whether this was healthy, etc. Or maybe he did, but he doesn't mention any of that in his lengthy post.

Research Does Not Support Tolerance Thesis

Atkinson believes that alcoholics are all characterized by his great tolerance for alcohol. But research does not support this idea. (For a common-sense counter-example, think of Native Americans, who have among the lowest tolerances for alcohol on earth, and among the highest alcoholism rates.) But here is something else he says is true of alcoholics, at least the ones he meets at AA: "every time I enter an Alcoholics Anonymous room, I am struck by a more or less uniform look of cosmic bafflement on the faces of my fellow addicts. *How in the world did this happen?*" (his italics).

Like Atkinson, they are mystified by their situation. Isn't that striking, after years and decades of drinking, drunkenness, hanging with people who pass out and in hard-drinking bars? I posted to my blog a description of my Life Process Program [LPP] for alcoholism and addiction as an alternative to the kind of uncontrollable, biological, disease model Atkinson posits. The LPP involves reviving people's values (like those Atkinson suppressed in those bars), rehearsing interpersonal and life skills (like communicating with people when you and they aren't intoxicated),

The Life Process Program for alcoholism and addiction involves such activities as practicing how to communicate with others when all participants in a conversation are sober.

and contemplating life issues and plans. I think addicts lack these things—just as Atkinson's post noticeably ignores them in his life.

Just in case you want to ask, "How many people testify that your approach saved their lives?", here's one that was . . . posted at my video on You Tube, Alcoholism Is Not a Disease: "The disease concept is a great excuse for poor choices! Alcoholism is not a disease and I am living proof of that. I read Stanton's book seventeen years ago and haven't touched a drop since that time." I'm glad for this man, just as I'm glad Atkinson is sober, at the same time that his comment shows that there are alternative approaches to Atkinson's. But it is on science, psychology, empirical effectiveness—as my blog entrée indicated—as well as on common sense that we must all rest our cases.

ELEVEN

The Drinking Age Should Be Lowered

John McCardell

In the following viewpoint John McCardell, the former president of Middlebury College in Vermont, argues that the drinking age should be lowered from twenty-one to eighteen. He argues that since alcohol has a permanent presence in American culture that cannot be legislated away, young adults should be taught how to make responsible decisions about alcohol use. He asserts that there is little evidence that raising the age of legal drinking to twenty-one has lowered alcohol-related traffic fatalities. Cracking down on underage drinking does not make young adults stop drinking, McCardell maintains; it only serves to make them drink in secret locations. He contends that the law mandating the drinking age as twenty-one should be changed.

It is time to rethink the drinking age. That's the message of nearly 130 college and university presidents who have signed on to the Amethyst Initiative, which declares that the 21 drinking age does not work and has created a culture of binge drinking on campus. While the initiative intentionally does not prescribe a specific new policy, it seeks a debate that acknowledges the current law's failure. (As a former college president, I am not a signatory, but I have helped spearhead the effort.)

The National Minimum Legal Drinking Age Act could not, constitutionally, mandate a national drinking age. Instead, it allowed the states to set the age as they chose. If, however, the age was lower than 21, the state would forfeit 10 percent of its federal highway appropriation.

End of debate. Until now.

As the discussion renews in earnest throughout the media and society, "science" will be used to support the status quo. Yet any survey of the evidence at hand shows that the data are peskily inconsistent. The National Institute on Alcohol Abuse and Alcoholism, a respected authority, believes that the 21-year-old drinking age works. Yet its website reveals that of 5,000 Americans under the age of 21 who die of alcohol-related causes

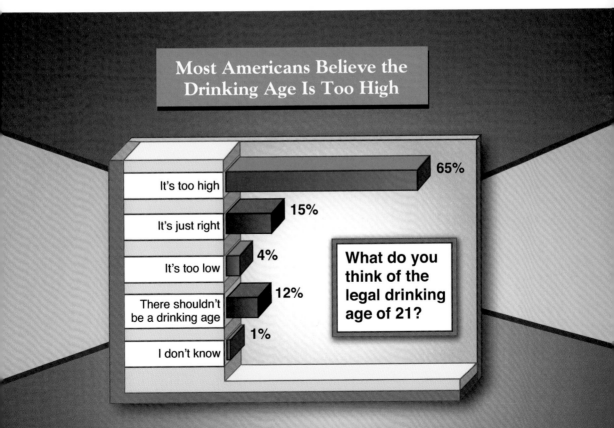

Most Americans Believe the Drinking Age Is Too High

It's too high	65%
It's just right	15%
It's too low	4%
There shouldn't be a drinking age	12%
I don't know	1%

What do you think of the legal drinking age of 21?

Taken from: Marc Fischer, "On Campus, Legal Drinking Age Is Flunking the Reality Test," *Washington Post*, August 21, 2008.

each year, only 1,900 are traffic fatalities, meaning the remaining 3,100 occur *off* the highways. Drunk teens behind the wheel are less of a problem than those drinking in private.

And drinking continues to be widespread among adolescents: The institute says that 75 percent of 12th graders, two thirds of 10th graders, and two fifths of eighth graders have consumed alcohol. Not surprisingly, the institute concludes that we have an "enormous public health issue." The Institute of Medicine notes that "more youth drink than smoke tobacco or use illegal drugs." The estimated annual social cost of underage drinking is $53 billion. These statistics will most likely not be offered in support of the current law.

Moreover, the evidence that raising the drinking age has been primarily responsible for the decline in alcohol-related traffic fatalities (a trend that effectively stopped in the mid-1990s and has been inching upward) is underwhelming. One survey of research on this subject revealed that about half of the studies looked at found a cause-and-effect relationship between the 21 drinking age and diminishing alcohol-related traffic fatalities— and half showed no relationship whatsoever.

Hidden Drinking. Yet college presidents are pilloried for daring to question our current laws. Even though many students who enter their institutions have already consumed alcohol, the presidents are labeled "shirkers" and "lawbreakers" for not enforcing an unenforceable law. The more they crack down on campus drinking, the more they simply force that behavior into clandestine locations, often off campus, beyond their sight and their authority.

Where, after all, does "binge drinking" take place? Not in public places, from which the law has effectively banned alcohol consumption, but in locked dorm rooms, off-campus apartments, farmers' fields, and other risky environments.

The "abstinence" message—the only one legally permissible— is failing, as prohibition has always failed. Presidents looking for a solution find such remarkable documents as the 2002 "Call to Action," written by a National Institutes of Health task force, which advises presidents to, in effect, break the law. It describes

Proponents of lowering the drinking age say that existing laws defining the legal drinking age do not stop teens from drinking in secret.

programs to "reduce," not eliminate, alcohol consumption. It recommends teaching "students basic principles of moderate drinking." In short, it advises what others have condemned.

Effective laws reflect not abstract, unattainable ideals but rather social and cultural reality. The reality in this case is that one is a legal adult at age 18; that alcohol is present in the lives of young adults ages 18 to 20; that most of the rest of the world has come out in a very different place on this issue; and that the 21-year-old drinking age is routinely evaded. Either we are a nation of lawbreakers, or this is a bad law.

TWELVE

The Drinking Age Should Not Be Lowered

Laura Dial

Laura Dial is the state executive director of Mothers Against Drunk Driving in Tennessee. In the following viewpoint Dial argues against lowering the drinking age to eighteen. She asserts that since states have raised the legal drinking age to twenty-one, the number of fatal drunk driving crashes has been reduced, saving more than twenty-five thousand lives. Dial foresees many potential problems if the legal drinking age is lowered: Alcohol will become even more pervasive on college campuses, and traffic fatalities among young adults due to drunk driving will increase.

We all know that binge and underage drinking are serious problems on our college campuses.

As executive director of MADD Tennessee, I have seen the devastating effects of underage drinking at our state's colleges and universities and on our roads. But lowering the drinking age is not the solution.

Unfortunately, more than 100 college presidents, including the president of Rhodes College, have chosen to address the issue by signing on to a misguided initiative aimed at lowering the drinking age from 21 to 18 years old.

The "21 Law" Saves Lives

The minimum legal drinking age is set at 21 because it has been proven to save lives by reducing the number of fatal drunk driving crashes caused by young drivers. Since the law went into effect in 1984, more than 25,000 lives have been saved.

As one of the most-studied public health laws in history, the scientific research from more than 50 high-quality studies all

European Youths Tend to Drink More than American Teens

Many people assume that European countries, which have a lower drinking age than the United States, are more successful than the United States at preventing heavy drinking among young people. However, surveys from those countries suggest otherwise. European adolescents who are below the legal drinking age tend to drink at higher rates than teens in the United States.

	France	Ireland	Italy	Sweden	United Kingdom	United States
Minimum drinking age	16	18	16	18	18	21
Had a drink, last 30 days	58%	73%	64%	51%	74%	35%
Had 5 or more drinks on at least one occasion (binge drinking) last 30 days	28%	57%	34%	37%	54%	22%
Been drunk at least once, last 30 days	15%	53%	19%	34%	46%	18%

Taken from: Center on Alcohol Marketing and Youth, "Prevalence of Underage Drinking," updated December 2007.

found that the 21 law saves lives. In addition, studies show that the law causes those under 21 to drink less and to continue to drink less throughout their 20s. The earlier youth drink the more likely they are to become dependent on alcohol and drive drunk later in life.

By lowering the age at which young adults are legally allowed to purchase alcohol, we are lowering the age of those who have easy access to alcohol and shifting responsibility for underage drinking to high school educators.

Parents understand and share this concern—72 percent of adults think lowering the drinking age would make alcohol more accessible to kids and nearly half think it would increase binge drinking among teens, according to a new Nationwide Insurance poll.

The Facts About Wisconsin

Proponents of lowering the drinking age to 18 have cited Wisconsin as an example of a state that allows people under 21 to drink legally in the presence of a parent or legal guardian.

They claim that this model of law will help parents teach their children to drink responsibly. Unfortunately, proponents of lowering the drinking age fail to cite the alarming underage drinking trends in Wisconsin.

According to the University of Wisconsin Population Health Institute, Wisconsin is the worst in the country in current drinking among high school students and current levels of underage drinking. Additionally, Wisconsin has the country's second-highest rate of underage binge drinking and fourth-highest percentage of traffic fatalities caused by drunk drivers.

Rhodes should revoke their support for the Amethyst Initiative for the safety of their students and their communities. We understand that there is no easy way to address the problem of underage drinking, but there are universities taking strong steps to enforce the 21 law and change the drinking culture in their campus communities.

We must continue to focus on the strategies that have shown the best results so far—sanctioning adults who provide alcohol to minors, changing the environment by tightening alcohol policies on campuses, as well as working with local establishments in college communities selling alcohol to sell responsibly and to ensure those under 21 are not being served.

Examine the Flaws in Logic

MADD's support of the 21 law is based purely on the science that proves that this law saves lives. However, if stats and numbers don't sway you, you can just examine the flaws in the logic of this proposal.

Mothers Against Drunk Driving believe that lowering the drinking age will result in more alcohol-related traffic fatalities involving young drivers.

If all college students are legally allowed to consume alcohol, are college-based parties really going to stop revolving around alcohol? Will keg parties feature root beer instead of beer? Will there be fewer bars in and around college campuses once the number of legal college age customers triples? Will bars have fewer happy hour promotions?

Clearly, few people would believe that these issues will change. This is because the real problem for college age students is related to the pervasive party culture that exists on many campuses. We need to target this culture and the university policies that support it to truly address this issue.

MADD welcomes an open discussion on how we can prevent the dangerous effects of underage and binge drinking—but the 21 law, a law that has been proven to save lives, is non-negotiable.

THIRTEEN

Alcoholics Anonymous Is Effective in Treating Alcoholism

Richard S. Sandor

> Richard S. Sandor is the author of *Thinking Simply About Addiction*, from which this viewpoint is taken. He argues that the Twelve-Step program of Alcoholics Anonymous (AA) is very effective in helping alcoholics stay sober. He asserts that most recovering alcoholics who start drinking again do so because they gave up on the AA program and forgot what they had learned about staying sober in the program. According to Sandor, relapses are not inevitable as long as the alcoholic stays true to the principles of twelve-step programs.

Recovery from addiction means more than quitting. It means, as AAs say, "staying quit." It means not beginning again. Once the difference between quitting and not starting again became clear to me, I began to interview patients in a new way. Rather than dwelling on why they had continued doing what was so obviously bad for them, I began to ask them if they had had any periods of abstinence and, if so, what they had been doing at the time.

What I discovered surprised me. If they hadn't been abstinent simply by "white-knuckling it," they had almost always been active in one of the 12-step groups (periods of enforced abstinence as a result of being in hospital or jail didn't count). I also learned that when they'd started using or drinking again, it was almost always *after* they'd stopped going to meetings, stopped talking with their sponsor, stopped working on the steps, or in some other way stopped actively participating in a good 12-step program.

Variations on Two Themes

After many years of listening to these stories, I began to hear them as variations on the same two themes: forgetting and not caring. If a patient had achieved a significant period of abstinence (on the order of months), he had begun drinking or using drugs again

According to the author, a proponent of the 12-step recovery program of Alcoholics Anonymous (AA), members who resume drinking have typically dropped out of AA.

in one of two ways: Either he forgot that, for him, there was no such thing as "just one" (drink, hit, snort, whatever), or else he knew it and had gotten into such a state of emotional distress that he didn't care.

Forgetting and not caring don't operate entirely separately, but for the purposes of thinking simply about how people begin again (and what they can do to avoid it), it's useful to note that they are different. The important point is that if a patient had become abstinent and then relapsed, it was almost always true either that he had never become active in a 12-step group or that he had been active and stopped going.

A Typical Story

A typical story of relapse by forgetting would go something like this:

"So, you say you were sober for how long last year?" I ask.

"Oh, about six months, I guess."

"What were you doing then . . . I mean, were you going to AA or anything?"

"Yeah, I was doing great there for a while, Doc. I was going to three meetings a week, and I was starting to work on my fourth step with my sponsor. At first my wife was real happy, but then it began to bug her that I was out at night so much. She even thought I was getting too friendly with some of the gals at the meetings."

"Was she going to her Al-Anon meetings?"

"Yeah, she was going for a while, but then she said the meetings were making her depressed, so she stopped going."

"What happened then?"

"Well, let's see. . . . Oh yeah, my sponsor had to move because of his job, so we kind of lost touch. Anyway, he was getting on my back 'cause I wasn't going to all the meetings he wanted me to. So, I just quit calling him."

"So how did you get started drinking again? I mean where were you when you had the first one? What were you thinking?"

"Let's see. . . . Oh yeah, I remember. Yeah, it was about six months after I went through the program. I was at a ball game with my buddy Mike. He was having a beer and offered me one. At first I said no, but then I thought, 'Hell, one beer won't hurt me.'"

"And when was that?"

"About a month ago. I don't know why I can't control it, Doc. I must have something real wrong inside. Maybe I'm just self-destructive. What do you think?"

"Were you thinking about 'destroying yourself' at the ball game when you had that beer?"

"Hell no! Are you crazy? I was having a good time, and I just had a couple that night. It really didn't get out of hand until the next weekend. That's when my wife and I had a big fight. I guess I forgot what I learned in the program."

Taking Your Medicine

This kind of forgetting isn't limited to people with addictions. If you think of going to meetings as "taking your medicine," then what this man told me is entirely consistent with what we find in medical practice generally: Only 26 percent of patients take their medications exactly as prescribed. We've all done it. You go to your doctor with a fever and terrible sore throat. She prescribes a course of penicillin lasting a week, suggests you take some aspirin, and tells you to rest for a while. A few days later your throat begins to feel better, and you jump back into your life. And then you forget to take the penicillin as it was prescribed. Two days later the infection comes back.

Lesson: It's hard to remember that something is wrong when nothing hurts.

Alcoholics Anonymous Helps Members Stay Sober

Every three years Alcoholics Anonymous (AA) randomly surveys its members to determine how long they have been sober. Its last survey, taken in 2007 of more than eight thousand members, found that on average, AA members have been sober more than eight years.

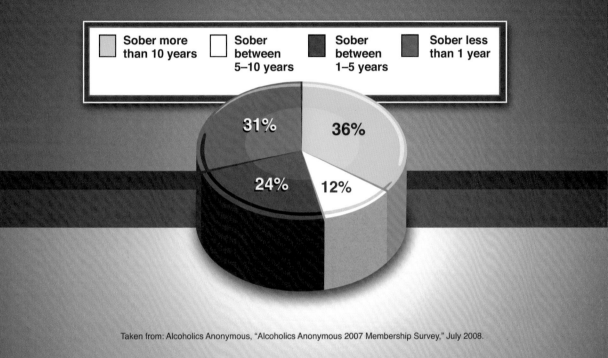

Taken from: Alcoholics Anonymous, "Alcoholics Anonymous 2007 Membership Survey," July 2008.

Translated to the problem of recovering from addiction, the same lesson goes like this: It's hard for people to remember how much they need their 12-step program when, as a result of having become sober, things start to get better. Relapse by forgetting is common only in the course of an addiction, before people are really convinced that their struggle for control is doomed to failure. More rarely, people forget after years of abstinence. In those cases, the culprit is complacency: People quit going to meetings and gradually forget what they had learned so many years before.

A Different Position

People who relapse as a result of not caring are in a different position. They may know very well that "there is no such thing as one" but are so beside themselves with grief, fear, shame, rage, or boredom that they simply can't stand it. If they think about it at all, their thoughts go something like this: "If this is how it feels to be sober, the hell with it. I was just as miserable when I was drinking; at least then I had a little relief."

A number of my patients who relapsed in this way were as perplexed as I was about how it had happened. They had been going to their 12-step meetings and had started drinking or using again anyway. How could that be? Eventually, as I learned to ask for specifics—the types of meetings they had been going to, whether they had been sharing at the meetings, if they had gotten a sponsor, what they had learned from the steps, if they had been of service, and so on—I nearly always found that they had not been participating wholeheartedly. *Why* they had been holding back then became the focus of the assessment and to a large degree shaped the treatment plan.

Emotional Triggers

The particular emotional "trigger" for starting up again can take many different forms—getting fired, having a fight with a spouse, becoming physically ill or depressed—all sorts of adverse events which the person simply can't cope with. But no trigger works without a spring. And in the case of the addict or alcoholic who isn't working a good 12-step program, that spring is being wound up tighter and tighter as time passes. Eventually, the slightest disturbance can set it off. AAs call it being a "dry drunk": behaving in all the destructive ways addicts and alcoholics typically behave but without actually drinking or using or, in other words, abstinent but not happy about it.

Treatment strategies aimed at helping people "stay quit" are lumped together in the category of "relapse prevention." I suppose that's acceptable as long as *relapse* isn't being used to describe something inherent in the addiction itself, as in the expression

"Addictions are chronic relapsing illnesses." Used in this way, the word *relapse* can imply that the patient is a helpless victim of the disease, as in the phrase "He *had* a relapse." Wrong. The only thing the patient *has* is the addiction itself. If he started again, it was something he *did*, not something that happened to him. Yes, after he began using or drinking again, something that has a life of its own took over, but that was *after* he chose to drink or use.

Twisting the Meaning of Relapse

When an addiction is described as a "chronic and relapsing brain disease," it can suggest to patients that no matter what they do, a relapse can still hit, as it were, "out of the blue." It supports the avoidance of responsibility and ultimately breeds a kind of self-serving fatalism. Not long ago, a man I was evaluating for a diversion program tried to twist the meaning of the word *relapse* in just this way, hoping to be excused for having chosen to use again. A cocaine-addicted physician, he said to me, "Come on. You're a doctor, you know this is a chronic relapsing disease." No, it is not. Addictions don't relapse; people relapse. Addicts and alcoholics must know from the outset of treatment that relapse is not inevitable, that it is possible and necessary to make choices and take actions that maintain sobriety. Isn't that obvious? If people couldn't choose not to drink or use again, how could anyone recover?

Of course, in simplifying the process of relapse down to forgetting and not caring, I haven't done justice to the complexities involved. Where mere ignorance ends and motivated forgetting begins is rarely clear, and the suffering that leads to relapse can range from trivial to profound, but the overall picture remains the same. More important, it provides a way of thinking about what the goal of treatment ought to be.

FOURTEEN

Alcoholics Anonymous Is Ineffective in Treating Alcoholism

Saint Jude Retreat House

> Baldwin Research Institute (BRI) is a nonprofit organization that researches, develops, and runs treatment programs (such as the Jude Thaddeus Home Program) for alcoholics and drug addicts. It argues that the success rates claimed by Alcoholics Anonymous (AA) and similar twelve-step programs are nothing more than made-up numbers and, in fact, produce results that are no better than undergoing no program at all. BRI further asserts that AA deliberately misleads the public about how successful its treatment program is. BRI also questions how AA's treatment program can be successful if its participants are told they can never get well because there is no cure for alcoholism. BRI believes a more effective program for alcoholics is one in which they are forced to take responsibility for their actions and are not allowed to use the excuse that they have an incurable disease to explain why the treatment failed.

Take an introspective look at your beliefs. You may say, "I still believe that alcoholism . . . is a disease. . . ." And if you do think that, you would be absolutely correct. Specifically, you did not say "alcoholism is a disease;" you said that you "believe" alcoholism is a disease. Your statement is correct because you are

Saint Jude Retreat House, "Hazelden and AA Statistics," 2007. Reproduced by permission.

stating a fact about yourself and not about whether alcoholism is or is not a disease. You, of course, are free to believe whatever pleases you as an individual. And, like . . . others, you have chosen a belief which is contrary to the empirical evidence and scientific method. To wit, you have chosen to ignore the facts in favor of a belief that better fits your personal wants or needs. A personal choice such as this needs no justification unless it in some way affects another negatively. By you and others around you buying into the absurd notion that drinking or drugging is a disease, you are constantly reinforcing the idea in your mind that you have this disease for which you are no longer responsible. If you have been "brainwashed" to the extent that the "disease of alcoholism" is firmly implanted in your psyche, then your chances of moderating or stopping drinking or drugging forever is minimal. Conversely, if you become willing to take full responsibility for your behavior, then your chances of stopping forever go up dramatically. . . .

Does Alcoholics Anonymous Work?

In its opening sentence of its preamble Alcoholics Anonymous [AA] claims that it "is a fellowship of men and women who share their experience, strength and hope with each other that they may solve their common problem and help others to recover from alcoholism." While this may be a good marketing strategy does it really help people? How effective is "sharing experience, strength and hope" in helping someone else and if it really is effective, where is the empirical data that proves the method? First, can sharing anecdotal information with someone else with similar problems be helpful? Please keep in mind that the entire program of Alcoholics Anonymous is based on anecdotal data, while the Jude Thaddeus Home Program is based entirely on 20 years of research. With that in mind consider the following:

While anecdotal accounts of individuals' successes and failures make for interesting reading, such reports can actually provide those attempting to change their lives with excuses for failure. These excuses come into play by way of a whole variety of thought processes (albeit unsound), however all the excuses emanate from a common source: comparisons. Stories about other substance abusers, unintentionally but inevitably, challenge the still using drug abuser to rationalize why he or she is not like the person in the story. Thus, if the Jude Thaddeus Home Program did rely on anecdotal reports, the substance abuser could firmly put in place the argument that the Jude Thaddeus Home Program may have worked for the person in the story, but I (the still using substance abuser) am different so there is no reason to believe that the program would work for me.

These rationalizations abound: I'm older; I'm younger. I'm male; I'm female. I'm white; I'm black. I'm from the city; I live in the country. I'm Irish; I'm German; I'm Russian; I'm Japanese; I drank a quart a day; I drink a pint a day; I drank at home; I am a bar drinker. I am a periodic; I drink daily. I'm a plumber; I am an engineer; I am a physician, I'm a truck driver. I am rich; I am poor. I had a good childhood; I had a horrible childhood, and so on, and so on. As you can imagine the number of permutations approaches infinity. Alternatively, substance abusers that are still using readily accept general information so long as the information is not personalized. This, then, is the methodology used in the Jude Thaddeus Home Program. The participant is presented with certain facts which allow him (her) to discover for themselves the nature and extent of their problem(s). The process of discovery is non-comparing and non-confronting.

In addition to the comparison problem, there exists a body of knowledge that definitively demonstrates the lack of success of anecdotal accounts as a method of helping substance abusers eliminate their substance abuse problem. Alcoholics Anonymous, for example, is a program based on its members' personal stories. The book entitled *Alcoholics Anonymous* is, on the whole, a regurgitation of AA members' stories. Actually, personal stories, autobiographical anecdotes, comprise 71% of the book. Twenty-nine percent of the book is claimed to provide a description of the "program of recovery." However, 54 of the 164 pages that claim to be the description of the program are, in fact, anecdotes (personal stories) to convince the reader of the effectiveness of the program. To wit, 33% of the program description is actually an anecdotal sales effort to get the reader to buy into the program. Thus and in aggregate, 80% of the book is anecdotal reports to convince the reader that the program works (or to sell books, which is not the same thing.)

AA's Results

So, what then, are the results achieved by anecdotal accounts of successes and failures. For that answer we turn to Alcoholics Anonymous General Services Office (AA GSO.) In 1990, AA

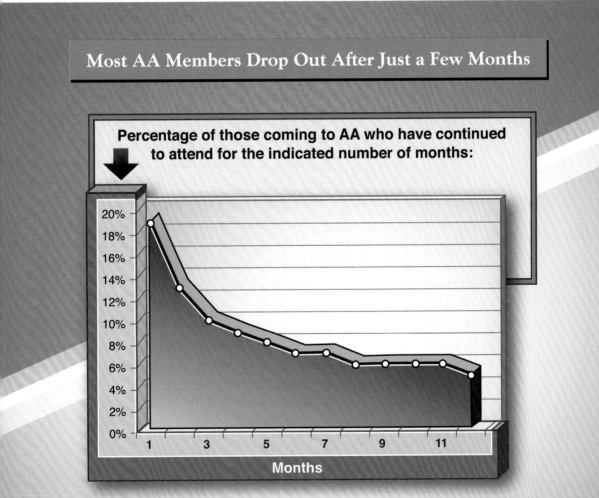

Most AA Members Drop Out After Just a Few Months

Percentage of those coming to AA who have continued to attend for the indicated number of months:

Months

Average of five surveys taken in 1977, 1980, 1983, 1986, and 1989

Taken from: Saint Jude Retreat House, "Hazeldon Treatment Center and AA Statistics," 2007.
www.soberforever.net/hazelden-treatment-center-and-aa-success-rates.cfm.

GSO, the governing organization overseeing all "autonomous" meetings, published an internal memo for the employees of its corporate offices. It was an analysis of a survey period between 1977 and 1989. The results were in absolute contrast to the public perception of AA: "After just one month in the Fellowship [meaning AA,] 81% of the new members had already dropped out. After three months, 90% have left, and a full 95% have disappeared inside one year!"

Based on this information it is reasonable, if not compelling, to conclude that anecdotal information given to substance abusers for the purpose of helping them stop drinking and/or drugging is ineffective and most researchers have since concluded that it is actually harmful. . . .

An Excuse for Failure

The disease theory provides substance abusers with a culturally accepted excuse for not taking responsibility for their own choices. Moreover, the 12 steps indoctrinate those who accept its teachings into a life devoid of personal accountability. . . . In this instance there is a plethora of rock solid evidence that the disease theory and the 12 step method fail 95% of the time and create *learned helplessness* in those 5% who are considered "successful."

Consider that the fundamental tenets of conventional treatment and Alcoholics Anonymous (pg. 60, *Alcoholics Anonymous*): ". . . make clear three pertinent ideas: (a) that we were alcoholic and could not manage our own lives, (b) that probably no human power could have relieved our alcoholism, (c) that God could and would if He were sought." The members of Alcoholics Anonymous and the professionals providing treatment services further reduce this propaganda for the abdication of personal responsibility to the following platitude: "I can't; He can; I think I will let Him." To wit, Alcoholics Anonymous and conventional treatment are based on individual powerlessness and abdication of all personal responsibility. . . .

All other programs available here in the US began as a program first, and more often than not, were based on the disease theory and the 12 step model. The disease theory and 12-step model grew into an amalgamation of fundamentalist Christian beliefs and pop-psychology known as the Minnesota Model. Subsequently, self-justifying research was conducted in an effort to justify these programs.

The Minnesota Model

Certainly, the Minnesota Model was a program first followed by self-justifying research. The Minnesota Model became the industry standard in 1949, but quite without efficacy studies until the mid 1980's. For more than 30 years the Minnesota Model did not know whether or not the program actually helped anyone. For the last 20 years the Minnesota Model claims it "has been monitoring treatment outcomes (how patients are doing after treatment) and our [meaning the Minnesota Model] data shows success." They report that "on average, 54% of our patients maintain an alcohol- and drug-free lifestyle during the entire year after treatment. An additional 35% significantly reduce their use. Between 70–80% report substantial improvements in the quality of their lives, with positive changes in relationships with family and friends, job performance, and the ability to handle problems. . . ."

The Minnesota Model success rate looks mighty familiar. Early AA statistics are reported in the book entitled *Alcoholics Anonymous*. In that book Page XV is the beginning of the foreword to the second edition. This foreword begins with the following notation: *"Figures given in this foreword describe the Fellowship as it was in 1955."* On page XX in the same foreword it states, "Of alcoholics who came to A.A. and really tried, 50% got sober at once and remained that way; 25% sobered up after some relapses, and among the remainder, those who stayed on with A.A. showed improvement. . . ." Practically speaking the success rate statistics quoted today by the Minnesota Model are statistically about the same as the statistics reported in 1955 by Alcoholics Anonymous.

Fundamental Flaws

There are, of course, some fundamental flaws in both sets of statistics which are either, intentional or unintentional, but in either case mislead the reader. Alcoholics Anonymous reports: "Of alcoholics who came to A.A. and really tried, 50% got sober at once." Significantly, Alcoholics Anonymous did not report "Of alcoholics who came to AA, 50% got sober at once." What Alcoholics Anonymous reported on was a subset of those who came to AA. Specifically, Alcoholics Anonymous reported *only* on those "who came . . . and really tried." Alcoholics Anonymous failed to tell the reader what criteria was used to determined those "who really tried" as opposed to "those who did *not* really try."

Next Alcoholics Anonymous asserts that ". . . 25% sobered up after some relapses. . . ." Again the reader is left without a definition for the phrase "some relapses." Alcoholics Anonymous does not describe what is considered a relapse. The term "relapse" seems harmless enough, but what if a member relapses once a week or every few days? And, what if this behavior extends over a period of 25 years or more? Often the relapser is between the ages of 40 to 60 years old when he (she) decides to stop drinking (and/or drugging.) Can Alcoholics Anonymous rightly take credit for an individual's triumph over substance abuse, when for 25 years Alcoholics Anonymous did not substantially affect the individual's drinking (and/or drugging) behavior.

Deceptive Claims

In more recent years studies have concluded that as a function of age, the probability increases for substance abusers to spontaneously stop their substance abuse, with or without the help of a program. That is to say, as substance abusers get older they are more likely to stop using alcohol and/or other drugs on their own. And finally, Alcoholics Anonymous does not identify the specifics with respect to its claim that "among the remainder, those who stayed on with A.A. showed improvement. . . ." The question, then, is: what constituted "improvement." Did they have better jobs? Did they manage their relationships better? Did they make more money and pay their bills on time? Did they enjoy better physical or mental health? Did they get into less trouble? Did they control their tempers better? Or was it perhaps all of these? Or, perhaps, it was none of these—perhaps it was determined that they showed improvement by the mere fact that they continued to show up at Alcoholics Anonymous meetings. Whatever the case, the real deception is not of an analytical nature. . . .

Misleading Claims

Alcoholics Anonymous' claimed success rate gives the reader the [illusion] that Alcoholic Anonymous has accounted for 100% of

According to the author, Alcoholics Anonymous provides only misleading and vague information about its success rate.

the population studied. This success would certainly be great news, if it were not so flagrantly fraudulent. Remember that Alcoholics Anonymous is actually reporting only on those "who came . . . and really tried." While we can not know exactly what the criteria was to distinguish between those who "really tried" and those who did not, it is reasonable to assume that those who came to Alcoholics Anonymous and who left shortly thereafter would probably have been counted among those who did *not* "really" try. Working with that assumption, based on Alcoholics Anonymous General Service Office graph that showed that within one year, of those who came to Alcoholics Anonymous during that year, 95% left Alcoholics Anonymous before the end of that same year. Thus, it would appear that those "who really tried" consists of 5% of the total within any given year. . . .

Dishonest Claims

There can be no doubt that the authors of the book *Alcoholics Anonymous* intended to mislead the reader by making their statistics sound like a 75% to 100% success rate. In a study conducted in 2006, we told 41 Baldwin Research Institute, Inc.'s employees in groups of 3 and 4 per group that they were required to study the book *Alcoholics Anonymous*. After reading the paragraph in the foreword of the second edition that gives the aforementioned statistics we ask each student what they understood the success rate of Alcoholics Anonymous to be. Of the 41 polled 35 thought the success rate, according to what they had just read, to be 75%. The other 6 had concluded that they had no idea because there was no way of knowing how big the population was that apparently did *not really try*. Of the 41 subjects polled, all but 1 were good readers with good to excellent comprehension. Slightly over 30% had college degrees and approximately 10% had advanced degrees. Yet more than 85% of the employees that read the paragraph accepted the statistical misinformation as fact. Accordingly there exists only two possibilities: (1) The authors of the paragraph did not know what they had done and were exceedingly "lucky" that what they had written was misunderstood to their benefit, or (2)

The authors knew exactly what they were doing and intended to deceive the reader into believing that the program of Alcoholics Anonymous is *20 times* more effective than it actually is.

After studying the book and the clandestine society of Alcoholics Anonymous for more than 25 years, it is clear that the AA authors intentionally deceived their readers. This conclusion is based on the fact that deceptions such as this one are repeated over and over again throughout the book. The point being that once might be a fluke; the same technique used a couple dozen times is deliberate. Moreover, it is dishonest.

FIFTEEN

Combining Alcoholics Anonymous with Clinical Treatment Is Effective in Treating Alcoholism

Helen Buttery

In the following viewpoint Helen Buttery discusses a study that found that people were more likely to stay sober if they received both clinical treatment and support from self-help groups, rather than just clinical treatment alone. Oftentimes, she writes, twelve-step programs (which usually advocate complete abstinence) are at one end of a continuum, while clinical treatment programs (which may permit drinkers to continue to drink in moderation) are at the other. Clinical treatment programs may get the alcoholic started on the road to recovery, Buttery writes, while the twelve-step program offers support in becoming and remaining abstinent. Buttery reports for the Canadian journal *CrossCurrents: The Journal of Addiction and Mental Health*.

Keith Humphreys, professor of psychiatry and behavioral sciences at Stanford University in California, won't win any popularity contests among colleagues for saying, "As educated professionals, we tend to look down on everybody." Yet it was one of the reasons why he found the results of his recent study so gratifying.

The two-year study, published in *Alcoholism: Clinical and Experimental Research* in 2007, found that individuals being treated for alcohol use issues had higher rates of abstinence when they received both clinical treatment and mutual aid support than cognitive-behavioural therapy alone. The study is challenging academic and clinical naysayers of mutual aid to rethink how they can help clients with alcohol problems, instead of dismissing mutual aid as separate from treatment or as having no scientific backing, as has often been the case.

Acknowledging the Benefits

Wayne Skinner, deputy clinical director of Addictions Programs at the Centre for Addiction and Mental Health in Toronto, says it's about time the value of mutual aid be acknowledged. "It's long overdue, but the whole area of mutual aid is being rediscovered by clinicians and it is being given a growing respect," he says. But why has it taken so long to get to this point?

For one, until relatively recently, there was no proof that mutual aid was effective, no benchmark study to validate the work being done by mutual aid groups. In the alcohol recovery world, Alcoholics Anonymous (AA) is the best known example. In an increasingly medicalized profession, 12-step programs and other forms of mutual aid are often dismissed by clinicians, who insist that providing effective treatment requires special training, says Humphreys. Mutual aid groups like AA, however, don't claim to provide treatment; rather, they offer support that can prevent relapse once treatment is over.

The value of being able to personally relate to each other's experiences, as having "been there," is often an essential part of

A two-year study found that people were more likely to stay sober if they received clinical treatment in addition to support from a self-help group such as AA.

the healing process for people with addictions, says Humphreys. "You don't need an advanced degree to work with 'I feel lonely,' 'I need some encouragement,' 'I need a hug.' Often mutual aid groups can meet those needs."

Ignorance and Arrogance

Humphreys is not alone in his thinking. "Doctors need an acute dose of humility," says Dr. Graeme Cunningham, director of the

Addictions Division at Homewood Health Centre in Guelph, Ontario. He points to two reasons for clinical resistance to working with mutual aid groups—ignorance and arrogance.

However, professional snobbery is not exclusively to blame. The disconnect also has roots in a divergence between the philosophies traditionally espoused by clinicians, who may take a harm reduction approach, and mutual aid, which tends to advocate abstinence. Traditional 12-step programs have been criticized for adhering to the rigid belief that alcoholism is a disease over which its victims are powerless. Critics say this undermines the influence of psychological factors, such as anxiety, and social factors, such as poverty, and disempowers people with alcohol use problems and other addictions. Others criticize 12-step programs, chiefly AA, for being white, religious, male-dominated and cultish.

An Outdated View

However, many argue, this is an outdated view of AA. Translated into 28 different languages, AA is found in Tehran, Dehli and San Paolo. Advocates argue that AA is simply a reflection of the people who attend the meetings. For those who still are not satisfied, alternatives to AA have emerged.

Where 12-step programs, particularly AA, have been accused of being too rigid, with no room for personal choice, clinicians have been criticized for being too soft. An abstinence goal is not necessarily a condition of treatment, and harm reduction strategies, aimed at increasing safety while the person continues to drink or drinking in moderation, are options. But experts say that despite these seemingly irreconcilable differences, treatment goals, from abstinence to harm reduction, can be seen as existing on a continuum, which opens the door to co-operation among services that have traditionally been seen as working at odds with one another.

"Increasingly, what has emerged is a more pluralistic perspective, which acknowledges that we need all of these things, and clients need to be offered treatments based on severity and motivation," says Skinner. In the United States, studies have found that half of those treated for alcohol and other substance use problems will be readmitted to treatment within two to five years.

Skinner sees mutual aid as a crucial component of the continuum of care for people who complete formal alcohol treatment. "Treatment has a finite span to it," he says. "The real challenge for people is living in the real world, and that's where mutual aid support may become essential." Mutual aid can be an invaluable support in preventing the relapse so common with alcohol dependence.

A Start on the Road to Recovery

Some may consider clinical treatment to be a softer approach, but it often gets people with alcohol problems started on the road towards recovery. "We meet people where they're at," explains Cunningham. In recovery himself for more than 20 years, Cunningham knows firsthand how important it is to have services available that are nonjudgmental and accessible. "I'd be dead now if people closed the door," he says.

More and more, addictions treatment is client-driven, with approaches to care existing on a continuum, or as Cunningham envisions it, an arc. Where people fall on the arc and what services are suitable is determined by many factors. For instance, a person who started drinking after the death of a loved one may require grief counselling. Or a person with both mental illness, such as bipolar disorder, and alcohol dependence may require concurrent treatment, which also includes attending a mutual aid group for people with bipolar disorder.

Where a person falls on the arc can also change over time. A person may not be ready to abstain from alcohol, but may decide later that sobriety is their goal. It also comes down to personality. Some people simply don't like groups. And there are cases where mutual aid may be detrimental. "We don't want mutual aid to be a deal breaker to treatment," says Skinner. He says that it's better that clients receive some professional treatment than no help. Skinner also says it is important that when treatment providers suggest mutual aid to clients, they must do so in a way that the client feels respected and not confronted.

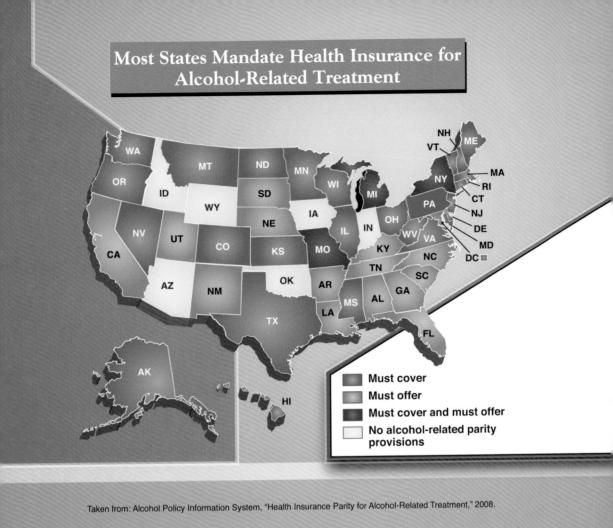

Most States Mandate Health Insurance for Alcohol-Related Treatment

Legend:
- Must cover
- Must offer
- Must cover and must offer
- No alcohol-related parity provisions

Taken from: Alcohol Policy Information System, "Health Insurance Parity for Alcohol-Related Treatment," 2008.

Suggestions Are Not Enough

But is suggestion enough? When clients are merely given information about mutual aid groups, which is the general practice among clinicians, clients don't seem to follow through. However, a 1981 study in the *American Journal of Drug and Alcohol Abuse* showed that when clinicians systematically encouraged clients to attend—by phoning the local AA, introducing the client to an AA member, having that AA member offer to meet the client before a meeting and giving a client a reminder the day of the meeting—100 per cent of clients attended and continued to attend.

But now, more than 25 years after that study, clinicians still are "not doing enough to encourage clients to attend mutual aid programs," says Humphreys. He says that it's not rocket science, but simply a matter of dealing with practical matters—Do they have a car to get to the meeting?—and other basic concerns clients might have—At the group, do they have to stand up and talk about their experience?

Humphreys puts himself in his clients' shoes and tries to address the types of questions or anxieties he himself might have if he were attending a meeting for the first time. "I try to answer all the questions I would have if I were going to an experience that was new and anxiety-provoking," he says. And if clinicians are not confident in their understanding of mutual aid groups, neither will their clients be.

What You Should Know About Alcoholism

Warning Signs of Alcoholism
- A craving—strong urge or need—for a drink
- A loss of self-control when drinking and an inability to stop drinking once the person has begun
- Drinking alone or in secret
- Blacking out or not remembering chunks of time
- Physical withdrawal symptoms when a person stops drinking, such as nausea, sweating, shaking, convulsions, and anxiety
- A high level of tolerance for the effects of alcohol and the need to drink more and more alcohol in order to achieve the same level of intoxication

Facts About Alcoholism
- A drink is defined as one 12-ounce bottle of beer or wine cooler; one 5-ounce glass of wine; or 1.5 ounces of 80-proof liquor.
- The effects of alcohol are noticed within ten minutes of taking a drink and peak within forty to sixty minutes of the first drink. If alcohol is consumed faster than it is metabolized by the liver, the blood alcohol content rises.
- About 18 million Americans, or 10 percent of the population, abuse alcohol or are alcohol dependent.
- Men are four times more likely to abuse alcohol than women.
- Young adults between the ages of eighteen and twenty-nine have more problems with alcohol than any other age group. Adults older than sixty-five are least likely to have alcohol problems.

- The earlier someone starts drinking, especially at age fourteen or younger, the more likely he or she is to abuse alcohol or to become alcohol dependent.
- Most college students (72 percent) started drinking while they were still in high school.
- Young adults tend to drink more once they arrive at college. In high school 26 percent of students have engaged in binge drinking, in which five or more drinks are consumed in one sitting. In college, 41 percent of students have participated in binge drinking.
- Women who are pregnant or trying to become pregnant should not drink alcohol, as the alcohol can harm the development of the fetus.
- People who are taking prescription medications should not drink alcohol, as the combination can have harmful interactions.
- Three oral drugs are used to treat alcohol dependence. Naltrexone reduces the craving for alcohol; disulfiram makes a patient physically ill if he or she drinks alcohol; acamprosate is used to help an alcoholic remain abstinent.
- Naltrexone, disulfiram, and acamprosate are never prescribed when an alcoholic is still drinking. These drugs are used to help a recovering alcoholic stay sober.
- Alcoholics Anonymous is the most well-known treatment program for recovering alcoholics, but it is just one of many self-help programs that try to help alcoholics become and remain sober.
- Relapses are common among people who are trying to stop drinking. One study showed that 86 percent of alcoholics entering a treatment program had a relapse within five years.
- More than one hundred thousand Americans die from alcohol-related causes each year. Examples include drunk driving, cirrhosis of the liver, accidents, and alcohol-related suicides and homicides.
- Alcoholics are at risk of developing liver and cardiac diseases.
- Alcoholics usually experience problems in their personal lives due to their drinking, such as job loss and estrangement from their families.

What You Should Do About Alcoholism

Many people, whether they are alcoholics or simply drink too much or too often, are reluctant to admit they have an alcohol problem. There is still a stigma attached to being an alcoholic that prevents some people from seeking help for their drinking problem. Others may claim they are not an alcoholic because they drink only on weekends or only after 5 P.M. or because they drink only wine or beer. However, someone can still be an alcoholic and drink only beer or wine or drink only on the weekends, in the evenings, or at certain events. If you suspect a problem, it is best to educate yourself about alcoholism and talk to an adult you trust, such as a parent, teacher, or counselor.

Understand Alcoholism

You should know the difference between someone who just likes to drink, and perhaps get drunk occasionally, and someone who is truly addicted to alcohol. It is especially important for you to recognize the signs of alcoholism if you are the one who is drinking. Talk to a responsible adult—a parent, teacher, school counselor, coach, or your religious leader, for example—about your concerns. Remember that most alcoholics will deny that they have a drinking problem, but if someone drinks alone or in secret, is not able to control how much he or she drinks, feels a need or compulsion to drink, and becomes upset if something interferes with his or her plans to drink, then this person may have a problem with alcohol.

In order to become informed, you should read as much as you can about alcoholism, its signs and symptoms, and its effects on the drinker's health and on his or her relationships with others. A good place to start is with the essays in this book. Librarians should be able to help you find other books, magazine articles, and Internet resources that will help you understand how alcohol can take control of someone's life. If you need an answer to a particular question about alcoholism, try to be as specific as possible during your Internet search, such as: "what are the warning signs of alcoholism," or "what are alcohol's effects on the body," or "how to treat alcoholism." When choosing Web sites to visit for more information, look at the Web addresses to make sure the sites are from reputable organizations. Visit the Web sites of the organizations listed in this volume to begin your search. When reading books, articles, and Internet information, try to determine what makes the author qualified to write about alcoholism and with which organizations the author is affiliated.

Alcohol Policies

Unless you are over the age of twenty-one, drinking alcohol is against the law. There are a few exceptions; for instance, if a minor (a person who is under the age of twenty-one) is drinking communion wine at a church service, if a minor is married to someone of legal drinking age, or if a minor is drinking in a parent's home with the parent's knowledge and consent. Parents who buy and supply alcohol for teen parties in their home are breaking the law in all fifty states, however.

Bars, restaurants, and stores that sell alcohol to minors can face fines and revocation of their business license or permit to sell alcohol. If you see someone under the age of twenty-one trying to buy alcohol, you should alert the manager, if you feel safe doing so. If you are at a party where underage drinking is going on, you should leave and inform either a responsible adult or the police. Whatever you do, do not let someone drive if he or she has been drinking. Take the keys away or call a parent or a taxi. Drunk driving (also known as driving under the influence—DUI—or driving while intoxicated—DWI) is a serious crime and often results in tragedy.

How to Help

If someone you know has a problem with alcohol, it may be difficult to convince him or her to seek help. Alcoholics tend to deny that they have a drinking problem. Talk to a trusted adult about the best approach for helping your friend or relative. Many support groups, such as Alcoholics Anonymous, are free. Those who attend the meetings do not have to tell their stories until they are ready to do so. Many insurance plans cover treatment for alcoholism in rehabilitation centers for periods ranging from just a few days to up to a month. Some treatment centers will take patients for even longer—three months or more—for those who can afford to pay out of their own pocket. In addition to support groups for the alcoholic, there are also support groups for those who are living with or affected by an alcoholic, such as Al-Anon or Alateen. Meetings are usually held in most communities at all times of the day. Local meetings can be found in the white pages of the telephone directory.

Examine Your Own Views

What motivates you? Under what circumstances might you drink alcohol? Would you drink alcohol to impress your friends? Would an honor code encourage you to refuse a drink? Would the possibility of being suspended from your sport or club or being expelled from school make you think twice about drinking? Do schools have the right to test for alcohol and drug use? Do the policies at your school seem to be working? Are other students in your school drinking? Decisions related to alcohol can be life altering. It is important to consider these and other questions surrounding the issue of alcoholism in order to make well-informed decisions.

ORGANIZATIONS TO CONTACT

The editors have compiled the following list of organizations concerned with the issues debated in this book. The descriptions are derived from materials provided by the organizations. All have publications or information available for interested readers. The list was compiled on the date of publication of the present volume; the information provided here may change. Be aware that many organizations take several weeks or longer to respond to inquiries, so allow as much time as possible.

Al-Anon Family Group Headquarters
1600 Corporate Landing Pkwy., Virginia Beach, VA 23454
(757) 563-1600 • fax: (757) 563-1655
e-mail: wso@al-anon.org
Web site: www.al-anon.alateen.org

Al-Anon is a fellowship of men, women, and children whose lives have been affected by an alcoholic family member or friend. Members share their experiences, strength, and hope to help each other and perhaps to aid in the recovery of the alcoholic. Al-Anon provides information on its local chapters and on its affiliated organization, Alateen. Its publications include the monthly magazine the *Forum*; several books, including *Discovering Choices*; and numerous pamphlets.

Alcoholics Anonymous (AA)
PO Box 459, New York, NY 10163
(212) 870-3400 • fax: (212) 870-3003
Web site: www.aa.org

AA is an independent, international fellowship of alcoholics who are sober or trying to become sober. Because AA's primary goal is to help alcoholics remain sober, it does not sponsor research or engage in education about alcoholism. AA members base their recovery on the Twelve-Step program. AA's catalog of publications include the books *Alcoholics Anonymous*, *Twelve Steps and Twelve Traditions*, the journal *AA Grapevine*, and the pamphlet *Is AA for You?*

Canadian Centre on Substance Abuse (CCSA)
75 Albert St., Ste. 300, Ottawa, ON K1P 5E7
(613) 235-4048 • fax: (613) 235-8101
e-mail: info@ccsa.com
Web site: www.ccsa.ca

The CCSA has a legislative mandate to reduce alcohol-related and other drug-related harms. It provides leadership on national priorities, is committed to advancing knowledge and understanding in the field, and is a leading partner in major national and international initiatives. It publishes the reports *Alcohol and Drug Use Among Drivers*, *Driving After Drinking in Canada*, and the quarterly newsletter *Action News*.

Hazelden Institute
PO Box 176, 15251 Pleasant Valley Rd.
Center City, MN 55012-9640
(800) 329-9000 • fax: (651) 213-4590
e-mail: info@hazelden.org
Web site: www.hazelden.org

The Hazelden Institute is a nonprofit organization dedicated to helping people recover from alcoholism and other addictions. It provides residential and outpatient treatment for adults and young people, programs for families affected by addiction, and training for specialists in addiction. The institute publishes the quarterly newsletter *Hazelden Voice*; the books *A Boomer's Guide to the Twelve Steps*, *Living Sober*, and *Choices and Consequences*; and numerous research updates about alcoholism.

Moderation Management (MM)
22 W. Twenty-seventh St., 5th Fl., New York, NY 10001
e-mail: mm@moderation.org
Web site: www.moderation.org

MM is a recovery program and national support network for people who are concerned about their drinking and who want to make positive lifestyle changes. MM empowers individuals to accept personal responsibility for choosing and maintaining their own paths, whether it is moderation or abstinence. MM promotes early self-recognition of risky drinking behavior, when moderate drinking is a more easily achievable goal. It offers on its Web site the pamphlet *Worried About Your Drinking?* and the book *Responsible Drinking: A Moderation Management Approach for Problem Drinkers*, as well as additional suggested materials.

Mothers Against Drunk Driving (MADD)
511 E. John Carpenter Frwy., Ste. 700, Irving, TX 75062
(800) 438-6233 • fax: (972) 869-2206
e-mail: info@madd.org
Web site: www.madd.org

MADD seeks to act as the voice of victims of drunk driving accidents by speaking on their behalf to communities, businesses, and educational groups and by providing materials for use in medical facilities and health and driver education programs. MADD publishes the quarterly magazine *MADDvocate*, numerous position papers, and a variety of brochures on drunk driving.

National Center on Addiction and Substance Abuse (CASA)
Columbia University, 152 W. Fifty-seventh St., New York, NY 10019
(212) 841-5200 • fax: (212) 956-8020
Web site: www.casacolumbia.org

CASA brings together all professional disciplines needed to study and combat substance abuse. The center informs Americans about the economic and social costs of substance abuse; assesses what works in prevention, treatment, and law enforcement; and removes the stigma of substance abuse. Publications include the books *High Society* and *Women Under the Influence* and the report *Wasting the Best and the Brightest: Substance Abuse at America's Colleges and Universities*.

National Clearinghouse for Alcohol and Drug Information

PO Box 2345, Rockville, MD 20847-2345
(800) 729-6686 • (301) 468-2600 • fax: (301) 468-6433
e-mail: shs@health.org
Web site: www.health.org

The clearinghouse distributes publications of the U.S. Department of Health and Human Services, the National Institute on Drug Abuse, and other federal agencies concerned with alcohol and drug abuse. It provides reports, fact sheets, posters, and videos on steroid abuse, prevention, and treatment. Some of the publications are available on its Web site; others may be ordered at low cost.

National Council on Alcoholism and Drug Dependence (NCADD)

244 E. Fifty-eighth St., 4th Fl., New York, NY 10022
(212) 269-7797 • fax: (212) 269-7510
e-mail: national@ncadd.org
Web site: www.ncadd.org

The NCADD provides education and information about, and help for, alcoholism to the public. It advocates prevention, intervention, and treatment through a national network of affiliates. In addition, it operates an information and referral line to educate and assist families and friends of alcoholics and drug addicts. It publishes fact sheets, such as *Underage Drinking* and *Youth and Alcohol*, and pamphlets such as *The Disease of Alcoholism* and *What Can You Do About Someone Else's Drinking?*

National Institute on Drug Abuse (NIDA)

6001 Executive Blvd., Bethesda, MD 20892-9561
(888) 644-6432 • (301) 443-1124
e-mail: information@nida.nih.gov
Web site: www.drugabuse.gov

The NIDA supports and conducts research on drug abuse—including the yearly Monitoring the Future Survey—to improve drug and alcohol abuse prevention, treatment, and policy efforts. It has Web pages devoted solely to alcohol abuse, where it offers research reports and information about alcohol. Information about alcohol abuse can also be found in its bimonthly *NIDA Notes* newsletter, the periodic *NIDA Capsules* fact sheets, and a catalog of research reports and public education materials, which can be found on the NIDA's home page at www.drugabuse.gov.

Rational Recovery Systems (RRS)
PO Box 800, Lotus, CA 95651
(916) 621-2667 • (916) 621-4374
e-mail: info@rational.org
Web site: www.rational.org

The RRS is a national self-help organization that offers a cognitive, rather than a spiritual, approach to recovery from alcoholism. Its philosophy holds that alcoholism is not a disease and that alcoholics can attain sobriety without depending on other people or a higher power. The RRS publishes the books *Rational Recovery: The New Cure for Addiction* and *The Triumph of Addiction* and numerous DVDs about its exclusive Addictive Voice Recognition Technique.

BIBLIOGRAPHY

Books

Rachel Brownell, *Mommy Doesn't Drink Here Anymore: Getting Through the First Year of Sobriety*. Berkeley, CA: Conari, 2009.

Roy Eskapa, *The Cure of Alcoholism: Drink Your Way Sober Without Willpower, Abstinence or Discomfort*. Dallas: Benbella, 2008.

Marcus Grant and Mark Leverton, eds., *Reducing Harmful Drinking: The Producers' Contribution*. New York: Routledge, 2009.

Jack H. Hedblom, *Last Call: Alcoholism and Recovery*. Baltimore: Johns Hopkins Press, 2009.

Charles Herrick and Charlotte A. Herrick, *100 Questions and Answers About Alcoholism*. Sudbury, MA: Jones and Bartlett, 2007.

Jeff Herten, *An Uncommon Drunk: Revelations of a High-Functioning Alcoholic*. Lincoln, NE: iUniverse, 2006.

George H. Jensen Jr., *Some of the Words Are Theirs: A Memoir of an Alcoholic Family*. Springfield, MO: Moon City, 2009.

Michael S. Levy, *Take Control of Your Drinking . . . and You May Not Need to Quit*. Baltimore: John Hopkins University Press, 2009.

Jerry Moe, *Understanding Addiction and Recovery Through a Child's Eyes: Hope, Help, and Healing for Families*. Deerfield Beach, FL: HCI, 2007.

Richard S. Sandor, *Thinking Simply About Addiction: A Handbook for Recovery*. New York: Jeremy P. Tarcher/Penguin, 2009.

Amy L. Sutton, ed., *Alcoholism Sourcebook*. 2nd ed. Detroit: Onmigraphics, 2007.

Doug Thorburn, *Alcoholism Myths and Realities: Removing the Stigma of Society's Most Destructive Disease*. Northridge, CA: Galt, 2005.

Trysh Travis, *The Language of the Heart: A Cultural History of the Recovery Movement from Alcoholics Anonymous to Oprah Winfrey*. Chapel Hill: University of North Carolina Press, 2009.

Harold Urschel, *Healing the Addicted Brain: The Revolutionary, Science-Based Alcoholism and Addiction Recovery Program*. Naperville, IL: Sourcebooks, 2009.

Periodicals

Anonymous, "Confessions of a Drunk Driver," *Ladies Home Journal*, November 2007.

Jessica Blatt, "My Drinking Problem Was Exposed on TV," *CosmoGirl!* June–July 2007.

John Cloud, "Should You Drink with Your Kids?" *Time*, June 30, 2008.

Stacy Colino, "How Partying Too Much Can Hurt You," *Cosmopolitan*, November 2007.

Karen Fanning, "An Addict's Life," *Scholastic Choices*, September 2008.

Mary Ferguson, "A Mother Under the Influence," *Parenting*, February 2007.

Linda Formichelli, "Is Alcohol Really Good for You?" *Health*, November 2007.

Timothy Gilsbach and Erin Gilsbach, "Re-evaluating First-Party Liability Under PA's Dram Shop Law," *Legal Intelligencer*, December 31, 2008.

Kendall Hamilton, "The Drunken Philosopher," *Esquire*, April 2007.

John Hastings, "Liquid Confidence," *O: The Oprah Magazine*, July 2007.

Paula Hunt, "Bottled Up: Family Emotions Go Haywire When Alcoholism Hits Home," *Current Health 2*, February 2009.

Karen Karbo, "Why Won't He Stop Drinking?" *Redbook*, June 2007.

Kevin R. Marciano, "A Holiday Gift to Reckless Bar Owners? Not a Good Idea," *Legal Intelligencer*, January 20, 2009.

Andrew Marshall, "Unhappy Hour," *Time International*, April 20, 2009.

John McCardell and Radley Balko, "Let My Students Drink," Reason Online, February 2009.

John J. Miller, "The Case Against 21," *National Review*, April 19, 2007.

Laura Dean Mooney, "A Lower Age Would Be Unsafe," *U.S. News & World Report*, September 8, 2008.

John I. Nurnberger Jr. and Laura Jean Bierut, "Seeking the Connections: Alcoholism and Our Genes," *Scientific American*, April 2007.

Nancy Doyle Palmer, "'You've Got to Stop,'" *Washingtonian*, February 2007.

Stanton Peele, "The Bizarre Effort to Eliminate Underage Drinking in the U.S.," *Addiction Research & Theory*, 2007.

Barbara Righton, "What's Too Much? Alcoholism Is Underdiagnosed," *Maclean's*, May 26, 2008.

Amanda Robb, "Hi, My Name Is Amanda . . . and I Might Be an Alcoholic," *O: The Oprah Magazine*, January 2007.

Darshak Sanghavi, "Quicker Liquor," *Slate*, August 26, 2008.

George Will, "Drinking Age Paradox," *Washington Post*, April 19, 2007.

INDEX